Sweets for Saints & Sinners

Sweets for Saints & Sinners

Janice Feuer

ILLUSTRATIONS BY
Veronica di Rosa

101 Productions, San Francisco

Published by 101 Productions
834 Mission Street
San Francisco, California 94103

Library of Congress Cataloging in Publication Data

Feuer, Janice, 1948-
    Sweets for saints and sinners.

    Includes index.
    1. Desserts.   I. Title.
TX773.F43   641.58'6   80-21934
ISBN   0-89286-180-0

Contents

JOIN ME FOR TEA 6
SUBSTANCE: BASIC PASTRIES & CAKES 14
INSIDE, OUTSIDE & ON TOP 26
MASTERPIECES 50
QUEEN OF TARTS 80
ON THE LIGHT SIDE 98
YEASTED & NOT 122
INDEX 140
BIOGRAPHICAL NOTES 144

Join Me for Tea

Come in and join me for tea. There is much to discuss, including many things you know intuitively already. I will go over a few of the basics I have learned through the years, though I do admit that much of what I do is more a result of feel or experience than a firm knowledge of facts. Thus, you are going to find recipes that give rounded baking times and "almost" quantities, or those that ask you "to taste" to make sure that you have created the flavor you want.

Even in the short time since this book was written, I have made changes in the recipes—adding orange zest here, ground nuts there. Don't hold me to the way I made something last week, just as I won't hold you to making these recipes exactly as I have written them. The exception to the latter is the first time you are making a dessert with which you are unfamiliar. Just "experiment" by following my directions. A wonderful bit of advice: You don't ever make anything wrong. This day's heavy cake becomes the reason why you know how to make tomorrow's cake feather light.

There are times when things around you affect your baking—the weather, your relationship with your lover, husband, wife or children, your job. Some days just won't be your days; your "baking chemistry" will be off. I used to have a week here and there of daily failures. Nothing tasted the way it could; it was just passable. And then, the next week everything seemed more delicious than I even knew it could be. Don't be discouraged. Failures creep into even the professional pastry chef's life.

One of the pleasures of being a pastry chef is having a different audience each night. Lacking that, be kind to your friends and family. No one needs to eat rich desserts every day, so experiment with some lighter sweets, fresh fruit or a bit of custard. Save your masterpieces for special times.

I have always found the preparation of desserts to be the most satisfying part of the meal. There is the pleasure of working with the ingredients—strawberries, chocolate, cream, almonds—and also the pleasure these ingredients give to those who consume the result. I am sure that part of my decision to become a pastry chef was knowing that people bestow the most loving praises upon the dessert maker. (I am also sure that this is part of the reason that it has always been difficult for me to follow a recipe exactly. Even if my addition of a teaspoon of cinnamon or a teaspoon of vanilla doesn't noticeably change the taste, I feel good because it becomes *my* recipe and I am thus worthy of the praise.)

My sweets odyssey is taking a new direction these days, a turn from light and sophisticated classical confections to humbler, less-refined delicacies guaranteed to please the eye and palate as well as to nourish the body and soul. This means substituting whole-wheat flour, fruit juices and honey for bleached flour, white sugar and corn syrup. Admittedly, the transition for me has been difficult. My palate was accustomed to "sweet," and at first, "less sweet" just tasted flat. Luckily, there were always "official tasters" to give their guidance and now there is a whole new world of ingredients with which to create.

The recipes that follow have been prepared and served in the various restaurants and kitchens in which I have worked over the past seven years. They were a result of the elements present on the day they were prepared: the ingredients for which they called were exactly the ones on hand, a special friend was coming to dinner and the dessert had to be special as well, or because an old standby would always come out a success no matter what my mood.

Thus, what I have included here is not meant to be a comprehensive survey of desserts, but rather just a few of my favorites and those for which I feel most proud.

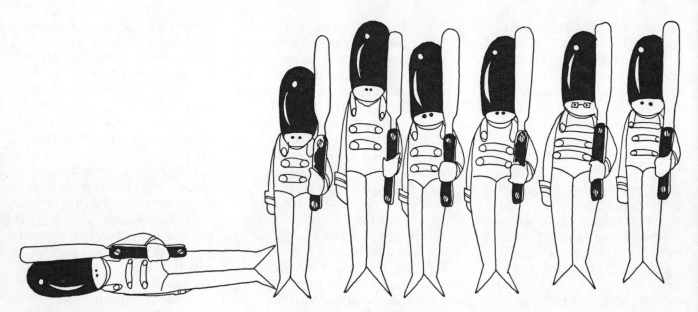

KITCHEN EQUIPMENT

Before you can begin delighting the dessert eaters in your life, it is helpful to have the proper equipment with which to work. There really aren't many things you need, and I suspect that many of them, if not all, are already part of your kitchen inventory. The following is a list of what has become essential for me.

• If you want to become a serious baker, a good *electric mixer* is a must. It should have a paddle (for creaming), whip and dough hook, making this kind of mixer more efficient than the hand-held variety. A mixer with metal bowls is ideal, as the bowls can do double duty as a double boiler.

• A *double boiler* makes "heat sensitive" ingredients, such as chocolate, less difficult to work with on the stove. It is a two-pan contraption, the bottom one for holding the gently boiling water that creates the heat for melting or cooking the ingredient in the top pan, which is suspended above the water. A *bain marie* is a similar setup: A metal bowl is placed in a pan of simmering water rather than over direct heat.

• An *electric blender* makes puréeing fruits or creating crumbs from your old cakes for patting onto the sides of your new cakes a pleasure. It is also good for grinding nuts, but you must be careful not to grind too long or your ground walnuts will become walnut butter.

• Two good, sharp *knives* are important. This means a professional chef's knife and

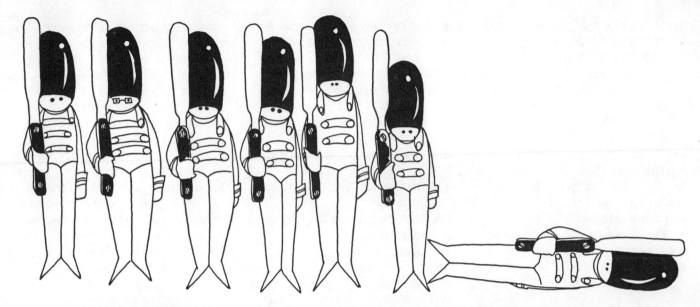

a paring knife. A *serrated-edged knife* with a 10- to 12-inch blade is necessary for cutting cakes into thin layers. A *palette knife* or *rubber spatula* is essential for smoothly masking cakes with whipped cream, frosting or mousse. A rubber spatula is also important if you are going to learn not to taste everything by "licking the bowl clean."

• A good *rolling pin* makes rolling out pastry dough a pleasure. I prefer one without handles, about 18 inches long and 2 inches in diameter.

• A *pastry scraper* is essential for cutting yeast bread or coffee-cake dough and pie pastry, as well as for cleaning your counter.

• *Accurate measuring spoons and cups*, preferably for both dry and wet measures, are important to the success of desserts. (And in this day, ones with metric equivalents so that you can adjust to the inevitable.) Dry measuring cups are flat on top and should be filled to heaping and leveled off. Wet measuring cups have pour spouts, with the line indicat-

ing the amount below the lip.

• A *wire sieve* is good for sifting both flour and sugar, as well as for straining seeds from berry purées.

• A *vegetable peeler* is handy for hulling strawberries or making chocolate curls.

• A specially designed *citrus grater* permits you to remove only the zest of the peel, leaving behind the white membrane. A standard kitchen grater will also work.

• A variety of *baking pans*: two or three 9-inch layer-cake pans, two or three 8-

inch layer-cake pans, one 9-inch square pan, one 9-inch spring-form pan, one 9- and/or 10-inch tube pan, one 11- by 16-inch jelly-roll pan, one or two standard-sized baking sheets, one 9-inch pie pan, one 10-inch tart pan or tart ring, five to eight 3-inch tart-let pans, muffin tins, one savarin mold, one dozen baba molds, two 9- by 5- by 3-inch loaf pans.

• Two or three heavy-bottomed *saucepans*, preferably graduated in size.

• *Mixing bowls* of various sizes, preferably metal.

• A reliable *stove* with a working oven, the temperature of which can be accurately measured. Buy a high-quality *oven thermometer* if you don't already have one. It is an indispensable addition to your kitchen.

• *Wire racks* are useful for cooling cakes, cookies and breads. An oven rack can also be used.

• *Parchment paper* is wonderful for lining pans, because it eliminates the somewhat messy buttering and

flouring process. Plus, parchment paper can be used to form cornucopias for decorating when your pastry bags are in use: Cut a triangle from the parchment paper and roll into a cornucopia, making a sharp, tight point at one end. Fill two thirds full with frosting or butter cream and fold over top so that the filling is pressed firmly toward the pointed end. With scissors, snip off pointed tip to form opening through which filling can be forced. Holding

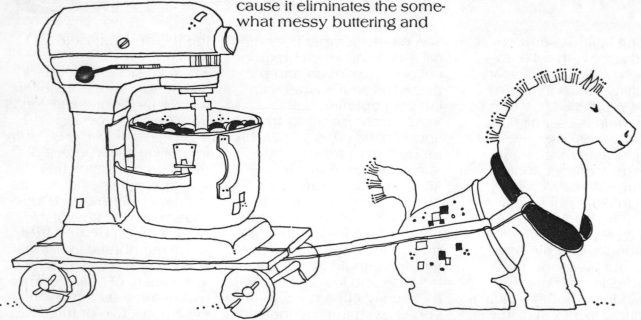

cornucopia one to two inches from item to be decorated, force filling out in pattern desired by evenly applying pressure to the top of the cornucopia.

- *Pastry bags* are indispensable for serious dessert makers. You will need two, 12 to 14 inches in length, and an assortment of plain and star metal tips. (A large pastry bag, about 20 inches in length, is handy for piping large quantities of cookie dough.) Pastry bags are good for a number of things: decorating cakes, forming cookies, filling cream puffs and cookies, etcetera. The tips are cone-shaped and have openings ranging in size from about 1/8 inch to 3/4 inch. The plain tips are generally used for filling pastries, shaping cookies or making cream puffs, eclairs, etcetera. The star tips are most commonly used for decorating cakes and pastries.

If you have not worked with pastry bags much, you will need to practice, perhaps with a malleable, inexpensive filling such as mashed potatoes, before you can achieve the beautiful results you want. First place the tip in the small end of the bag by dropping it through the top, making sure it protrudes from the bottom. Fill the bag two thirds full and twist the top securely against the filling so that it is pressed down into the tube. Using your right hand (if you are right handed), apply pressure on the top of the bag so that the filling is forced out through the tip. At the same time, use your left hand to direct the lower end of the bag. As the filling level begins to drop, retwist the top to maintain the pressure. For simple rounds, such as cookies, hold the bag vertical to the surface on which you are forming the round, about 1/4 inch from it. Apply pressure, forming a round in the size desired, then release the pressure and move the bag away. To make mounds, raise the bag slightly before releasing the pressure. Rosette shapes are made in the same way as mounds, but using a star tip. With practice, you will be able to make a variety of sizes and shapes with ease.

BASIC INGREDIENTS

Just as your kitchen must be outfitted with basic equipment for dessert making, so too must your shelves hold a number of staples. You should keep the following on hand.

- *Flour:* All purpose and unbleached white, whole wheat and whole-wheat pastry, and cake.
- *Chocolate:* Unsweetened, semisweet and unsweetened Dutch-type cocoa.
- *Eggs:* These recipes have been tested with Grade A large eggs. I have been lucky enough to find a source for fresh ranch eggs, which make an unbelievable difference in color and taste. (A tip: Substitute two yolks for each whole egg in coffee cakes for extra richness and nicer texture.)
- *Butter:* I use both unsalted butter and lightly salted butter. Most of the recipes simply call for butter, which refers to the lightly salted variety.
- *Nuts and seeds:* Try to purchase whole nuts and seeds and grind, chop or

slice them yourself for better flavor. I suggest you lightly toast all of your nuts or seeds (page 48) before using them as it improves their flavor. Keep almonds, walnuts, sunflower seeds, poppy seeds and sesame seeds on hand. Pecans, pine nuts and hazelnuts are nice for special occasions.

• *Yeast:* I prefer active dry yeast in the powdered form over cake yeast, which is more perishable. Keep them both refrigerated and be sure to check the expiration date on the package before using.

• *Baking soda and double-acting baking powder:* Again, check the expiration dates.

• *Vanilla extract:* Use only *pure* vanilla extract. *Never* use imitation vanilla flavoring (or any other imitation flavoring, such as almond, maple, etcetera). The flavor is recognizable as "off," and will adversely affect the natural flavors it is combined with. I love the flavor of vanilla and use it frequently, often in combination with liqueurs to round out their flavors. I do not use vanilla bean, though it also provides a pure flavor. Of course, continue to use vanilla bean if it is your present practice.

• *Liqueurs:* Use your favorites. I often specify a liqueur in a recipe, though any one can usually be substituted. To get a stronger liqueur flavor without diluting your mixture, burn off the alcohol in the liqueur, which reduces its quantity by more than

half. You can then get twice as much flavor to volume.

• *Sugar, honey and malt syrup:* Granulated white sugar, light or dark brown sugar and confectioners' sugar are all important to classical baking. Honey is not always interchangeable for sugar, since the latter adds not only sweetness but also a distinctive color and flavor. Honey adds different kinds of texture and flavor, and can be substituted for sugar in some recipes by using half as much honey as sugar indicated. Some cooks also reduce the amount of liquid called for in the recipe by a tablespoon for each quarter cup of honey used. The flavor of honey, that is, whether strong or light, is determined by the color of the honey. The darker honeys have a stronger flavor. Malt syrup, made from barley and with a texture like honey, is about 80 percent as sweet as honey, has its own distinctive taste and is particularly lovely in breads.

• *Yoghurt, sour cream and kefir cheese:* Plain yoghurt can sometimes be used in place of the liquid called for in a recipe, as can sour cream. I have a friend who always uses sour cream in place of butter in a *génoise*. Kefir cheese, a relatively new product in this country, has a thick, sour cream-type texture and a taste similar to cream cheese.

Substance:
Basic Pastries & Cakes

The recipes in this chapter are the "basics." Once you have mastered the techniques for creating these cakes and pastries, your innovative career as a dessert maker has begun. A few alterations on flavorings, on fillings, on nuts or on flours, and *voilà*—a "new dessert."

BASIC PIE CRUST

This is my favorite. It is a basic pie crust that is easily prepared with an electric mixer and can be made with all-purpose or unbleached white or whole-wheat pastry flour. This recipe also lends itself to the making of a large number of crusts at one time. The advantage of making crusts in quantity is that you may form the pastry on tins and then stack and freeze the unbaked shells for up to two months in a regular freezer or up to one month in a frost-free one. The freezing process actually produces a flakier result when the crust is baked. It is important, however, that you have a *heavy-duty* mixer that can handle quantity.

You must allow your pastry to determine its own water "needs." On some days your pastry will be "thirsty," while other days it will drink up only a little of the water you have provided.

For One 9-inch Crust
1/4 pound butter, or
   5 tablespoons butter and
   3 tablespoons margarine
1 cup flour (see introductory note)
2/3 teaspoon salt
2 tablespoons water

*For Two or Three
9-inch Crusts*
1/2 pound butter, or
   10 tablespoons butter and
   6 tablespoons margarine
2 cups flour (see introductory note)
1/2 tablespoon salt
1/4 cup water

*For Twelve to Sixteen
9-inch Crusts*
2 pounds butter
1 pound margarine
3 quarts (12 cups) flour
   (see introductory note)
2 tablespoons salt
3/4 cup water

Place the butter in your electric mixer and beat until creamed but not light and fluffy. (You do not want to beat air into the butter.) Add the flour and salt and mix at medium speed until *crumbly*. Continue mixing at medium speed while you count to 10, then *stop*. Remove the pastry from the bowl and transfer to a sheet pan, leaving any water remaining in the bowl unless the pastry feels and/or looks dry. If the latter condition exists, work in the water. Cover dough with plastic wrap and refrigerate at least 1 hour before rolling the dough out. (The dough will be easier to handle if it is rolled out the same day it is made. If this is not possible, allow it to sit in the refrigerator for up to 1 week.) Allow the dough to come to room temperature before attempting to roll it out. Follow directions for rolling out and prebaking given on page 18-19.

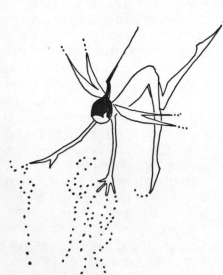

GINGER-COOKIE CRUST

4 tablespoons butter
2 cups ground Ginger
  Cookies, page 120
1 cup ground lightly
  toasted walnuts

Cream the butter and mix in the ground ginger cookies and walnuts until well blended. With your fingertips, press the mixture onto the bottom and sides of a 9-inch spring-form pan. If specified in recipe, prebake as directed on page 18-19.
Makes one 9-inch crust

GRAHAM-CRACKER CRUST

4 tablespoons butter
1/2 cup firmly packed
  brown sugar
1/2 cup granulated white
  sugar
2 cups finely crushed
  graham crackers
1 cup ground lightly
  toasted almonds
1/2 teaspoon ground
  cinnamon

Cream the butter and mix in the sugars until well blended. Then mix in the crushed graham crackers, almonds and cinnamon. With your fingertips, press the mixture onto the bottom and sides of a 9-inch spring-form pan. If specified in recipe, prebake as directed on page 18-19.

Any crust mixture that is leftover can be refrigerated in a tightly covered container for up to 2 weeks. To use, bring to room temperature and place in a mixing bowl. Whip by hand or on the low setting of an electric mixer until the butter softens.
Makes one 9-inch crust

OATMEAL-HONEY CRUST

This is an excellent alternative to a graham-cracker crust. It is especially nice with Avocado Pie.

2 cups rolled oats
1/4 cup whole-wheat pastry
  flour
1 teaspoon ground cinnamon
1/4 pound butter, melted
  and cooled
1/4 cup honey
1 cup lightly toasted sliced
  almonds or whole
  sunflower seeds

Combine the rolled oats, pastry flour and cinnamon and mix well. Stir in the butter and honey. When well blended, add the almonds or sunflower seeds and mix well. With your fingertips, press the mixture onto the bottom and sides of a 9-inch spring-form pan. If specified in recipe, prebake as directed on page 18-19.
Makes one 9-inch crust

SWEET PASTRY
(Pâte Sucrée)

This pastry is most suitable for tarts in which the crust is completely prebaked before filling with fresh fruit. The pastry is very delicate and will easily become soggy, thus you must not fill these tart shells more than a few hours before serving them. You must also be careful not to let the pastry brown too much in the oven. Any left-over pastry can be used for making delicious sugar cookies.

1 scant cup all-purpose or
   unbleached white flour
Pinch of salt
4 tablespoons butter,
   at room temperature
1/4 cup granulated white
   sugar
2 egg yolks
2 drops vanilla extract

Sift together the flour and salt onto a pastry board, forming a large ring and leaving the center free for the remaining ingredients. Put the butter, sugar, egg yolks and vanilla extract in the center of the ring, and with the fingertips of one hand, mix the ingredients together until well blended. With a spatula or pastry scraper, quickly draw in the flour to form a non-sticky ball of dough that holds together. It may not be necessary to incorporate all of the flour, or you may need to add more flour to achieve the desired result. Knead lightly with your fingertips until the dough is smooth. Wrap in plastic wrap and refrigerate for 15 minutes. Roll out, fit into a tart pan or tartlet pans, chill and line with beans or rice according to general directions on page 18-19. Bake in a preheated 375°F oven for 15 minutes, or until the crust just begins to color and is cooked through.
Makes one 9- or 10-inch tart shell or five or six 4-inch tartlet shells

ROLLING OUT AND PREBAKING PIE CRUSTS

Bring the dough to room temperature (75°F). If it is too cold, it will crack while you are rolling it out. Working with only enough dough to make 1 full crust or 3 to 5 tartlet shells at a time, place it on a *lightly* floured board. (Too much flour will make a dry, floury crust.)

Shape the dough into a ball and then flatten it with the palm of your hand into a 1/2-inch-thick round. With a lightly floured rolling pin, begin rolling out the dough. Always roll at right angles to the last roll. To do this, make one good roll just to the edge of the round, turn the dough to the left 45 degrees and roll again. Continue until you have formed a circle approximately 12 inches in diameter. Before each turn, pat the edges of the circle together with the sides of your hands to prevent cracking. To facilitate turning the dough, gently slide a long-bladed knife underneath the pastry to pre-vent it from sticking to the board. If the pastry begins to stick, place a little flour underneath it and rub a little flour on your rolling pin.

To transfer the pastry to a pie tin, overlap the circle onto your rolling pin, lift it and place it on the tin. Gently ease into place, especially into the corners. If you are using a straight-sided tart pan, trim off the edges by rolling the pin across the top edge to cut off the overhanging pastry. If you are using a pie tin, press the dull side of a knife blade against the pastry at a slight angle to the tin's edge. Any tears in the pastry can be patched by applying a small bit of egg white and covering the holes with a little piece of the pastry trimmings. Chill the prepared crusts for at least 15 minutes before baking, or wrap, stack and freeze for up to 2 months.

To partially bake the shells, line with a piece of aluminum foil or parchment paper. Fill with uncooked beans or rice and bake in a preheated 375°F oven for about 15 minutes. To test if the crust is ready, lift the foil or parchment, and if no pastry sticks to it, remove the crust from the oven. Remove the beans or rice and lining and reserve for use another time. Then fill the pie shell and bake according to the recipe's directions.

To completely prebake the shell, proceed as above to the point where you remove the beans or rice and lining. Return to the oven and continue to bake until a light golden brown. Fill according to the recipe's directions.

CHOU PASTRY
(Pâte à Chou)

A wonderfully easy pastry to master. It forms the base for many entrées and hors d'oeuvre, as well as dessert confections such as éclairs, cream puffs and profiteroles. This recipe differs from others for *pâte à chou* in its use of light cream for the usual water. I find that the cream makes a better, softer crust. Experiment. Make one batch with cream, a second with water and choose for yourself. Once I even used buttermilk with good results.

1/4 pound butter
1 cup half-and-half cream
1 cup all-purpose flour
4 or 5 eggs

Preheat the oven to 375°F Line a baking sheet with parchment paper or lightly butter and flour.

Combine the butter and light cream in a saucepan. Place over medium heat and bring just to boiling, then add the flour all at once. With a wooden spoon, stir rapidly until the mixture forms a ball in the center of the pan. This should take from 3 to 5 minutes. Remove the saucepan from the heat and transfer the pastry to the bowl of an electric mixer. With the mixer set at medium speed, add the eggs, one at a time. Add the fifth egg only if the mixture is not the proper consistency, that is, if it will not form a peak when the beaters are withdrawn from it.

With a pastry bag fitted with a plain round tube (1/2 inch in diameter for small pastries and 3/4 inch in diameter for large pastries), pipe the pastry onto the prepared pan into the desired size and shape depending on use. Place in the preheated oven and bake until golden brown and puffed. Stick a trussing needle or the tip of a small-bladed knife into the side of each pastry. Turn the oven off and leave the pastries in it until they are completely dried out, about 10 minutes for small ones, 15 to 20 minutes for medium-sized ones and 30 minutes for the largest ones. *Makes 80 to 90 small pastries, 25 to 30 medium-sized pastries or 10 large pastries*

GENOISE
(French Sponge Cake)

The *genoise* is the most versatile of the French cakes, the basis for a seemingly endless number of delicious desserts. It is a thin cake, which typically gets cut horizontally in halves or thirds for filling and frosting. If you prefer a taller cake, make two or more *genoise* for a four-, six- or eight-layer masterpiece.

As there is no baking powder or soda in this cake, the lightness comes from the proper whipping of the eggs and folding in of the flour and butter. You must take care to do this final step rapidly so as not to deflate the glorious egg mixture. Experiment with the type of flour you use—all-purpose or unbleached white, pastry or whole-wheat pastry.

For One 9-inch Cake
4 eggs
1/2 cup granulated white
   sugar
2/3 cup *sifted* flour
4 tablespoons butter, melted
   and cooled
3/4 tablespoon vanilla
   extract or liqueur of choice

For Two 8-inch Cakes
6 eggs
3/4 cup granulated white
 sugar
1 cup *sifted* flour
6 tablespoons butter,
 melted and cooled
1-1/4 tablespoons vanilla
 extract or liqueur of choice

*For One 11- by 16-inch
Jelly-Roll Pan*
5 eggs
2/3 cup granulated white
 sugar
3/4 cup *sifted* flour
5-1/3 tablespoons butter,
 melted and cooled
1 tablespoon vanilla extract
 or liqueur of choice

Line with parchment paper
or butter and flour the appropriate pan(s). Preheat the
oven to 350°F.

In a large metal bowl, combine the eggs and sugar
and, with a wire whisk, stir a
few times. Place the bowl in
a *bain marie* or over the bottom pan of a double boiler
containing about 2 inches of
water. Set over medium heat.
Whisk the egg-sugar mix-
ture rapidly until it is warm
to the touch and the sugar is
dissolved. (If using a *bain
marie*, you must whisk *very
rapidly* so the eggs do not
begin to cook. Heating the
mixture helps to whip the
eggs to a greater volume.)
Immediately remove the
bowl to an electric mixer
and beat at high speed for 5
to 15 minutes (depending
upon the mixer's efficiency)
until tripled in volume and
thick. The mixture should be
very light and fluffy and almost have the appearance
of whipped cream. (If you
are without an electric mixer,
beating with a rotary beater
will require 20 to 30 minutes to attain this result.)

With one hand, gently fold
in the flour, butter and vanilla
extract or liqueur. Using your
hand for folding assures your
knowing if there are any
undispersed lumps of flour or
pools of butter remaining at
the bottom of the bowl. If you
prefer, you may use a rubber
spatula for this step. Pour the
batter into the prepared pan(s)
and bang the pan(s) lightly on
a table or counter top to
remove any air bubbles.

Bake the cake(s) in the preheated oven for 20 to 25
minutes, or until the edges are
slightly pulled away from the
pan sides and the top(s) are
lightly browned and springy
to the touch. Immediately turn
out of the pan(s) and cool on a
wire rack. Allow to cool completely before using. These
cakes can be made in advance
and, when cooled, wrapped
airtight for a stay in the refrigerator of several days or in the
freezer for up to 2 months.

CHOCOLATE GENOISE Substitute
sifted unsweetened cocoa
powder for half of the flour.
Proceed as directed, using
vanilla extract alone or in
combination with rum, orange-
flavored liqueur, brandy, Káhlua,
etcetera.

LEMON OR ORANGE GENOISE Substitute fresh orange or lemon
juice for the vanilla extract or
liqueur. Add the grated zest
from 1/2 orange or 1 lemon to
the batter when adding the
flavoring.

CRUMB CAKE Substitute fine
crumbs made from leftover
cookies, cake or muffins for
half of the flour and flavor as
desired.

CHOCOLATE CAKE FOR ROLLING

6 ounces semisweet
  chocolate
2 tablespoons double-
  strength brewed coffee
6 eggs, separated
1 teaspoon vanilla extract
3/4 cup granulated white
  sugar
2 tablespoons flour
Granulated white sugar

Line an 11- by 16-inch jelly-roll pan with parchment paper. Preheat the oven to 375°F.
  Combine the chocolate and coffee in the top pan of a double boiler and melt over gently simmering water. Remove from the heat and

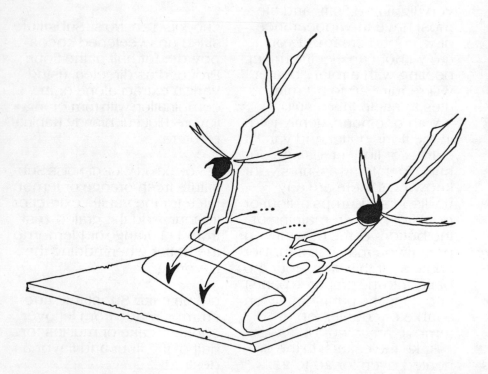

whisk in the egg yolks and the vanilla extract. Whip the egg whites until they form soft peaks. Then add the sugar, 1 tablespoon at a time, and continue to beat until stiff peaks form. Gently fold in the flour and the chocolate-egg mixture and pour into the prepared pan. Smooth the batter evenly in the pan with a rubber spatula.

Bake for 10 minutes in the preheated oven, then reduce the heat to 350°F and bake another 5 minutes, or until the top is firm and springy to the touch. Remove from the oven, place on a wire rack and allow to cool to room temperature in the pan.

Sift granulated sugar evenly over a piece of parchment paper about 1 inch larger in dimension than the jelly-roll pan. Loosen the edges of the cake with a knife blade and turn out onto the prepared parchment paper. Fill according to the recipe you are preparing: Bûche de Noël, Chocolate Roll, Chocolate Cream Roll, etcetera.

Makes one 11- by 16-inch cake

SAVARIN DOUGH
(For babas au rhum, savarins and petits savarins)

1 tablespoon active dry yeast
2 tablespoons granulated white sugar
1/4 cup lukewarm water (110° to 115°F)
2 eggs, beaten
1/2 teaspoon salt
4 tablespoons butter, melted and cooled
2 cups all-purpose or unbleached white flour

In a large mixing bowl, combine the yeast, sugar and water, stir to dissolve and let stand until foamy. Mix in the eggs, salt, butter and flour.

Knead the dough in the bowl by cupping one hand and lifting and slapping the dough against the sides of the bowl for 5 to 8 minutes. The dough is sufficiently kneaded when it is no longer sticky and has enough elasticity to enable you to stretch it into a 12-inch length and twist it without its breaking. Form the dough into a ball,

cover the bowl with a lightly dampened towel and set it in a warm place until double in bulk, about 1 hour.

Punch down the dough and fill a buttered 9-inch savarin ring or approximately 12 buttered individual baba molds or muffin-tin wells 2 inches deep by 2 inches in diameter. To fill the savarin mold, pick off small pieces of the dough (1 to 2 table-spoons in size) and slightly overlap them in the mold. To fill the molds or muffin-tin wells, divide the dough into approximately 12 equal portions, form the portions into balls and place the balls in the molds. In either case, the ring or molds should be no more than one half to two thirds full. Cover and let rise again in a warm place until almost double in bulk. Bake in a preheated 375°F oven for 15 minutes for baba molds and 30 to 35 minutes for a savarin mold, or until nicely browned. Remove from the oven and let cool slightly before turning out onto a wire rack.

Makes one 9- inch savarin or 12 babas

MERINGUES

For years I avoided making meringues. I assumed I would fail at the task. Then the day came when I could put off making them no longer. What a pleasant surprise. Now that I knew how to whip egg whites and how to use a pastry bag properly, there was nothing in the process left to fate.

There are several things you must know to successfully make meringues. You must begin with utensils completely free of grease and the egg whites at room temperature. The first addition of sugar must be made very gradually, beginning when the egg whites lose their yellowish color, turn white and are able to hold soft peaks. When the whites hold stiff peaks, have lost their sheen and are no longer grainy to the touch, the remaining sugar is folded in very carefully, using a rubber spatula.

Once the egg-white mixture is piped onto baking sheets in the desired sizes, the meringues are placed in a preheated 250°F oven. Because meringues are not so much baked as allowed to "dry out," they should be baked for 15 minutes, then, with the oven turned off, allowed to remain there for from 4 to 6 hours to overnight. Alternatively, they can be baked for 15 minutes, the oven then turned off for 30 minutes, then turned back on for 15 minutes, then off again, on again, until the meringues are completely dry, can be easily lifted from the baking sheet and their bottoms are firm. You must be careful never to allow the meringues to color. (The exception to this: Once, when an "accident" caused my meringues to tan, we changed the name to "chestnut meringues" and they became a house favorite.) To store, wrap well and freeze up to a month, or keep in a dry, airy container for several weeks.

Included here are a basic meringue recipe and my favorite one for fancy cakes and other desserts, Meringue Japonaise.

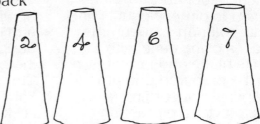

BASIC MERINGUE

1 cup egg whites
  (approximately 10)
2 cups granulated white
  sugar

Preheat the oven to 250°F. Line 3 baking sheets with parchment paper or lightly butter and flour.

Beat the egg whites until they form soft peaks. Gradually add 1 cup of the sugar, 1 tablespoon at a time. Continue beating until the egg whites hold stiff peaks, have lost their sheen and are no longer grainy to the touch. Fold the remaining cup of sugar into the egg whites with a rubber spatula.

Transfer the mixture to a pastry bag and pipe it onto the prepared pans, using a plain or star tip about 1/2 inch in diameter. Make the meringues in the diameter desired by starting in the center and pressing out a continuous pencil-width-thick strip, forming a tight coil in the shape of a circle.

Bake in the preheated oven as directed in the introduction. *Makes three to five 9-inch meringues*

MERINGUE JAPONAISE Follow directions for Basic Meringue, reducing the second 1-cup sugar measure to 3/4 cup. Sift together 2 tablespoons cornstarch and the 3/4 cup sugar and then mix in 1/4 cup ground lightly toasted almonds, walnuts, hazelnuts or nuts of choice. Fold this mixture into the stiffly beaten egg whites and proceed as directed.

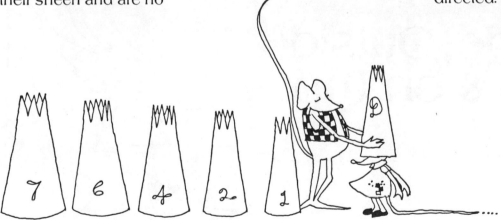

Inside, Outside
& on Top

This is another chapter of "basics." The mastery of a French butter cream will make you look forward to every special occasion as a chance to "perform" in the kitchen. You will discover how wonderful frostings can taste—no longer granular and simply sweet, but rich, smooth and flavorful. Cake and pastry fillings will take on new dimensions: Most anything whipped into cream cheese is delightful to consume. Fresh fruit layered thickly by itself or with whipped cream makes for light cakes, beautiful when cut and served. Lemon or chocolate mousse can fill or mask a masterpiece. Some desserts need the unifying effect of a sauce to most luxuriously blend their flavors and textures. Or a sauce can turn the simple dish of ice cream into something special. Your desserts need no longer be mundane. The frostings, fillings, sauces, preserves and garnishes presented here can make the commonplace extraordinary.

RED CURRANT JELLY GLAZE

This glaze and the apricot one that follows are most often used to lightly coat the fruit of a fruit tart. Which one you use depends upon the color of the fruit you are glazing: This glaze is suitable for red or dark-colored fruits, such as plums, strawberries, raspberries, cherries, blueberries, etcetera. For yellow or light-colored fruits, such as pineapples, bananas, oranges, apples, pears, use the Apricot Glaze.

These glazes may be kept almost indefinitely in the refrigerator. To use, heat just to the boiling point.

1 cup red currant jelly
2 to 4 tablespoons Kirsch, Cognac, Grand Marnier or liqueur of choice

Combine the jelly and liqueur in a small pan and heat slowly just to the boiling point. Use while hot.
Makes approximately 1 cup

STRAWBERRY GLAZE Substitute strawberry jelly for the red currant jelly.

APRICOT GLAZE

You may use the least expensive apricot jam you can find to make this glaze, as it is strained before use.

1 cup apricot jam
1 tablespoon fresh lemon juice, or
2 to 4 tablespoons Kirsch, Cognac, Grand Marnier or liqueur of choice

Combine the jam and lemon juice or liqueur in a small pan and heat slowly just to the boiling point. Put through a wire strainer and use while hot.
Makes approximately 1 cup

CITRUS GLAZE

Perfect for coffee cakes, such as Swedish Tea Wreath.

1-1/4 cups confectioners' sugar
1/4 cup fresh orange, lemon or lime juice
1 teaspoon vanilla extract
Grated zest of 1 orange

Combine all of the ingredients and mix until smooth. Drizzle on cakes still warm from the oven.
Makes approximately 1-1/4 cups

HONEY-ORANGE GLAZE

Use on coffee cakes, or perhaps on a carrot cake you don't want to frost.

2 tablespoons honey or malt syrup
1 teaspoon vanilla extract
5 tablespoons non-instant dry milk
1 tablespoon butter
Grated zest of 1 orange

Combine all of the ingredients in the top pan of a double boiler. Heat, stirring, over gently simmering water until smooth. Drizzle on cakes still warm from the oven.
Makes approximately 1/2 cup

CHOCOLATE GLAZE MADE WITH SEMISWEET CHOCOLATE

Excellent for coating éclairs, dipping strawberries, glazing cakes or for black bottom pie.

4 ounces semisweet chocolate
2 tablespoons coffee essence,* Grand Marnier, rum, Kirsch, Cognac, Amaretto or liqueur of choice
1/4 pound unsalted butter

Combine the chocolate and liquid in the top pan of a double boiler. Place over gently simmering water until melted, then remove from the heat. Stir in the butter, a tablespoon at a time. The mixture should be very smooth and slightly thickened, that is, capable of coating a spoon without dripping. Use while hot.

This glaze refrigerates well. To use, reheat in the top pan of a double boiler, remove from the heat and stir in a tablespoon or more of butter until glaze is once again the proper consistency.
Makes approximately 3/4 cup; enough for glazing the top and sides of an 8-inch cake

*To make the coffee essence, dissolve 2 tablespoons instant coffee powder in 2 tablespoons boiling water.

CHOCOLATE GLAZE MADE WITH COCOA POWDER

Perfect over ice cream for the ultimate hot fudge or black and tan sundae, or use in any of the ways specified for Chocolate Glaze made with Semisweet Chocolate, preceding.

1 cup *sifted* unsweetened dark cocoa powder
2/3 cup heavy cream
5-1/3 tablespoons unsalted butter
1-1/3 cups granulated white sugar
1/2 tablespoon vanilla extract, and/or
1 tablespoon liqueur of choice

Combine the cocoa powder, cream, butter and sugar in a saucepan placed over low heat. Cook, stirring constantly, about 5 minutes, or until very smooth and slightly thickened. Stir in the vanilla extract and/or liqueur. Use while hot.

This glaze refrigerates well. To use, reheat in the top pan of a double boiler, remove from the heat and stir in a tablespoon or more of butter until glaze is once again the proper consistency.
Makes approximately 1 cup; enough for glazing the top and sides of a 9-inch cake

CHOCOLATE-CREAM CHEESE FROSTING

A friend in Canada wrote me of a frosting made with chocolate, cream cheese and honey. This is my version— quickly made and lovely with banana cake, Gâteau Montmorency or as a spread on pound cake at tea time.

4 to 6 ounces semisweet
    chocolate*
2 tablespoons double-strength
    brewed coffee or liqueur or
    fruit juice of choice
1 pound cream cheese, at
    room temperature
1/3 cup honey, warmed
1 teaspoon vanilla extract

Combine the chocolate and coffee, liqueur or fruit juice in the top pan of a double boiler. Heat over gently simmering water just until melted. While the chocolate is melting, cream together the cream cheese and honey until smooth. Mix in the melted chocolate and the vanilla extract until thoroughly blended.
Makes enough to fill and frost an 8-inch, 2-layer cake

*The amount of chocolate you use will depend on how chocolatey you wish the result to be.

30

MERINGUE-BASE FRENCH BUTTER CREAM

2 egg whites
1/2 cup granulated white
 sugar
1/3 cup *sifted* confectioners'
 sugar
1 tablespoon vanilla extract
2 tablespoons margarine
1/4 pound plus 4 table-
 spoons unsalted butter

Put the egg whites and granulated sugar in a metal bowl and set over the bottom pan of a double boiler. Beating constantly with a wire whisk, heat over simmering water until the mixture is hot, approximately 120°F. Immediately remove the bowl from the heat and whip the mixture with an electric mixer until thick and cold, about 10 minutes. Gradually add the confectioners' sugar while continuing to beat. Reduce the speed to low and beat in the vanilla extract and the margarine and butter, a table-spoon at a time. Continue to beat until smooth and fluffy. *Makes enough to cover the top and sides of an 8- or 9-inch cake*

NOTE If the butter cream begins to curdle, heat a complementary liqueur or fruit juice to boiling and beat into the butter cream, a teaspoon at a time, until smooth.

CHOCOLATE BUTTER CREAM Alternating with the vanilla extract, margarine and butter, beat in 4 ounces semisweet chocolate melted with 1/4 ounce unsweetened chocolate and 1 tablespoon double-strength brewed coffee.

MOCHA BUTTER CREAM Dissolve 6 tablespoons instant coffee powder in 3 tablespoons boiling water. Melt 4 ounces semisweet chocolate with the brewed coffee and beat in alternately with the vanilla extract, margarine and butter.

PRALINE BUTTER CREAM Alternating with the vanilla extract, margarine and butter, beat in 1 cup crushed Praline, page 49, and 3 tablespoons Cognac, rum or orange-flavored liqueur, warmed.

CHESTNUT BUTTER CREAM Prepare the French Butter Cream, substituting 3 tablespoons rum or Cognac, warmed, for the vanilla extract or added in addition to the vanilla extract. Beat in 1 cup chestnut purée alternately with the flavoring, butter and margarine. The chestnut purée may be obtained in any one of the following ways: Simmer peeled fresh chestnuts in milk to cover until soft, then put through the fine blade of a grinder or purchase a jar of *marrons glacés*, drain well and put through the fine blade of a grinder. You can also purchase chestnut purée in a can—*marrons aux naturels*.

CUSTARD-BASE CHOCOLATE BUTTER CREAM

This butter cream uses egg yolks rather than whites. It is a wonderful alternative to the recipe on the back of the confectioners' sugar box and is easily made with honey.

4 ounces semisweet
  chocolate
3 tablespoons coffee
  essence*
4 egg yolks
1-3/4 cups granulated white
  sugar, or
  1 cup honey
1/2 cup water
1/2 pound unsalted butter

Combine the chocolate and coffee essense in the top pan of a double boiler. Place over gently simmering water until melted, then remove from the heat and set aside. Beat the egg yolks until pale and fluffy; set aside. Combine the sugar or honey and water in a heavy saucepan, bring to a boil and boil until the temperature reaches 238°F on a candy thermometer (soft-ball stage). This temperature is very important: If the mixture is too hot, the butter cream will crack and be unwieldy; too cold and the butter cream will be too soft. Dribble this syrup into the beaten egg yolks, beating constantly with an electric mixer set at the highest speed. Reduce the speed to medium and slowly beat in the melted chocolate. Reduce the speed to low and blend in the butter, a tablespoon at a time.

Makes enough to cover the top and sides of an 8- or 9-inch cake

*To make the coffee essence, dissolve 3 tablespoons instant coffee powder in 3 tablespoons boiling water.

NARSAI DAVID'S CUMBERLAND RUM BUTTER

Especially for plum pudding. Narsai found that the substitution of brown sugar for the white in his original recipe gave a more flavorful rendition of this classic accompaniment.

1/2 pound butter
1 cup firmly packed brown
  sugar
3/4 teaspoon ground
  nutmeg
3 tablespoons cream sherry
2-1/2 tablespoons dark rum

With an electric mixer, cream together the butter, brown sugar and nutmeg. Gradually mix in the sherry and rum. Turn the mixer to high speed and whip until fluffy. Do not worry if the mixture begins to separate. Just continue to whip and the emulsion will take place.

Makes 1-1/2 to 2 cups

EGG-CUSTARD SAUCE

Use this sauce in place of the traditional hard sauce over steamed plum or persimmon pudding.

6 egg yolks
1/2 cup granulated white
 sugar
1/3 cup brandy

Combine all of the ingredients in the top pan of a double boiler. Place over gently boiling water, and with a wire whisk, whip until the mixture begins to thicken. Serve at once.
Makes approximately 1 cup

HARD SAUCE

1/4 pound unsalted butter
1-1/8 cups confectioners'
 sugar, sifted
2 tablespoons brandy, or
 to taste
1/2 teaspoon vanilla extract

Cream the butter until fluffy. Add the sugar and continue creaming until very light and fluffy. Mix in the brandy and vanilla extract.
Makes approximately 1 cup

RASPBERRY PUREE

I prefer to use frozen rather than fresh raspberries for this recipe, as they result in a richer color and flavor when prepared in this manner. Plus, what a horrible thing to do to fresh raspberries, usually so scarce and thus so precious.

This is a wonderful sauce for many desserts, either spooned on top or as a shallow pond under individual servings. Try it with Chocolate Decadence, Almond Cake, cheesecake or Chocolate Roll.

Any amount of frozen
  raspberries

Purée the raspberries in a blender. Strain through a sieve.

FRESH STRAWBERRY SAUCE

A beautiful color because of the addition of frozen raspberries. Quite nice with Crème Renversée or cheesecake.

2 cups hulled strawberries
2 tablespoons confectioners'
  sugar, or to taste
2 tablespoons Grand Marnier
1/2 cup puréed and strained
  frozen raspberries

Pick through the strawberries, reserving 1 cup of the nicest ones. Leave these reserved berries whole if they are small, or halve or quarter them if they are large. Place them in a serving bowl.

Put the remaining cup of strawberries in a blender container and add the sugar, Grand Marnier and raspberries. Blend until smooth, taste and add additional sugar if necessary. Pour over the strawberries in the serving bowl.
*Makes approximately
1-1/2 cups*

APRICOT SAUCE

An easy-to-prepare sauce for cheesecake, ice cream or pound cake that can be jazzed up with the addition of a liqueur. I once added a little raspberry purée and some Grand Marnier for a beautiful reddish-orange sauce. On another occasion I tossed in a banana and a bit of brandy during the puréeing stage. The result each time was delicious.

3/4 cup dried apricots
1-1/2 cups unsweetened
   apple juice
1/3 cup honey
Additional apple juice or
   liqueur of choice, as needed

Combine the apricots and apple juice and let stand overnight. Transfer the apricots and apple juice to a saucepan and add the honey. Cook over low heat, uncovered, for 30 minutes. Transfer to a blender container and purée until smooth. If necessary, add additional apple juice or liqueur of choice to create the right consistency—pourable and capable of lightly coating a spoon.

This sauce may be used either warm or cold. Store refrigerated in a container with a tightly fitting lid for up to 2 weeks.
Makes 2 cups

PEACH SAUCE Substitute dried peaches for the apricots.

CARAMEL SAUCE

The other half of the ultimate black and tan sundae, or a glaze for a special cake.

3/4 cup granulated white
   sugar
2 tablespoons light corn
   syrup
1/4 cup water
6 tablespoons unsalted
   butter
1/3 cup heavy cream
2/3 cup lightly toasted sliced
   almonds

Combine the sugar, corn syrup and water in a neavy saucepan. Place over low heat, and stirring constantly, heat until the sugar and corn syrup are dissolved. Raise the heat and cook until it turns a deep golden color, wiping down the sides of the pan with a pastry brush dipped in cold water and being careful the mixture does not burn. Stir in the butter and cream and bring to a boil. Mix in the almonds.

Store in a tightly covered container in the refrigerator. To reheat, place in a double boiler.
Makes approximately 1 cup

STRAWBERRY-NUT BUTTER

1 basket strawberries, hulled
1/2 cup honey
2 tablespoons fresh lemon
   juice
12 tablespoons butter, at
   room temperature
1/2 cup finely ground lightly
   toasted almonds, walnuts,
   hazelnuts or pecans

Purée the strawberries and put them into a small saucepan. Add the honey and simmer, uncovered, stirring occasionally, for 25 minutes. Stir in the lemon juice, then cool to room temperature.
   Beat the butter until softened. Then beat in the cooled strawberry mixture and the nuts. Transfer to a container with a tightly fitting lid and refrigerate until hardened. This butter will maintain its freshness in the refrigerator for up to 2 weeks.
Makes approximately 2 cups

VARIATIONS Substitute for the strawberries 1-1/2 cups puréed raspberries, blackberries, peaches, apricots or plums.

SPICED ORANGE SYRUP

The first chef I ever worked for suggested adding bay leaves to the liquid used for poaching oranges. It proved a perfect addition, filling out the range of flavors. The syrup tasted so good that it became my favorite one for lacing cakes.

1 cup granulated white
   sugar, or to taste
2 cups water
4 whole cloves
4 whole allspice
2 large bay leaves
1 lemon, halved
1 orange, halved

In a heavy saucepan, dissolve the sugar in the water over low heat, stirring constantly. Bring to the boil and boil for 5 minutes. Add the cloves, allspice, bay leaves, lemon and orange, lower the heat and simmer, uncovered, for about 1 hour. Taste for strength. (Too much reduction will result in a bitter-tasting syrup.) Strain into a container with a tightly fitting lid for storage. This syrup will last for several weeks under refrigeration before changing flavor or spoiling. Use while cool.
Makes approximately 1 cup

CHEESECAKE SPREAD

This cream-cheese spread is so named because basically it is cheesecake without the eggs. It was created for accompanying Cranberry-Nut Bread at a Christmastime buffet, but has since done honors with other tea breads all through the year.

1/2 pound cream cheese, at
   room temperature
2-1/2 tablespoons honey
1 teaspoon granulated white
   sugar
1/4 teaspoon freshly grated
   lemon zest
Dash of vanilla extract

Combine all of the ingredients in a mixing bowl and blend until creamy and spreadable.
Makes approximately 1 cup

STREUSEL

A lovely topping for pies or coffee cakes.

4 tablespoons butter
1/4 cup firmly packed
   brown sugar
1/4 cup granulated white
   sugar
3/4 cup all-purpose or
   unbleached white flour
Grated zest of 1 orange
1 teaspoon ground
   cinnamon
1/2 cup chopped lightly
   toasted walnuts

Cream together the butter and white and brown sugars. Mix in the flour, orange zest, cinnamon and walnuts just until the mixture is crumbly. To store, place in a tightly covered container in the refrigerator for up to 1 week. Longer storage will cause loss of flavor.
Makes approximately 2 cups

PASTRY CREAM

This rich custard, which the French call *crème pâtisserie,* is just as custard should be—full of flavor and the richness of eggs and cream. Serve with fresh fruit or as the base for a fruit tart

2 cups half-and-half cream
1/2 cup all-purpose or
　　unbleached white flour
1/4 teaspoon salt
3/4 cup granulated white
　　sugar, or
6 tablespoons honey
8 egg yolks, beaten
1-1/2 tablespoons vanilla
　　extract
2 tablespoons butter

In a heavy saucepan, combine 1/2 cup of the half-and-half cream and the flour. Stir with a whisk until smooth. Gradually whisk in the remaining cream, the salt and sugar or honey. Cook over medium heat, stirring constantly with a wooden spoon so that none of the mixture thickens unattended along the sides of the pan. When the mixture thickens, stir a little of it into the yolks, then pour the yolks into the pan, whisking them in well. Be careful not to allow the mixture to come to the boil. Cook the mixture over low heat for another minute until it thickens a bit more. Remove from the heat and stir in the vanilla extract and butter. Strain through a sieve into a container with a tightly fitting lid. Store up to 1 week in the refrigerator.
Makes approximately 3 cups

APRICOT-BANANA FILLING

Use to fill coffee cakes, such as Bienstitch, between cake layers or on hot toast or bagels.

1 cup dried apricots,
　　chopped
1 cup unsweetened apple
　　juice
1 ripe banana, mashed
1/2 pound cream cheese, at
　　room temperature
1/4 cup honey
1/2 cup lightly toasted
　　walnuts or nuts of choice,
　　coarsely chopped

The night before you wish to use this filling, place the apricots and apple juice in a small saucepan. Cook over high heat for 2 minutes. Remove from the heat and stir in the mashed banana. Cool to room temperature and store covered in the refrigerator overnight.

The next day, beat the cream cheese with an electric mixer until smooth. Beat in the honey and then the apricot-banana mixture. Mix in the nuts.
Makes approximately 3 cups

ALMOND-CHEESE FILLING

Use this as a layer on which to set strawberries, raspberries or even cranberries for tarts with prebaked shells. It is also nice for dipping berries, or as a filling, with the addition of a tablespoon of flour, for Cheese Kuchen.

6 ounces cream cheese
4 ounces almond paste
Grated zest and juice of
  1/2 lemon
1-1/2 teaspoons Kirsch or
  Grand Marnier
1/2 teaspoon almond extract

Cream together the cream cheese and almond paste until smooth. Add the lemon zest and juice, Kirsch or Grand Marnier and almond extract and blend in well.
*Makes approximately
1-1/4 cups*

LEMON CURD OR LEMON FILLING

An English favorite and mine, too. It has just the right amount of tartness to make your mouth pucker a bit. Excellent on toast or at tea time, or let it cool in the bowl and fold in whipped cream to create a lemon mousse. Pour the filling while it is still hot into a prebaked tart shell, let it cool and set and you have a delicious lemon tart. It is also lovely as a filling for cakes, such as Gâteau au Citron.

5 egg yolks
Grated zest and juice of 2
  lemons
1/2 cup granulated white
  sugar
4 tablespoons butter

Place the egg yolks, lemon zest and juice and sugar in a metal mixing bowl and set the bowl in a *bain marie* of gently boiling water. With a wire whisk, whip rapidly and continuously until the mixture becomes thick and light. Remove the bowl from the *bain marie* and, bit by bit, whisk in the butter. Ladle into a sterilized 1-cup jar with a tightly fitting lid and refrigerate.
Makes approximately 1 cup

NOTE This recipe may be increased proportionately if a larger quantity is desired.

OLD WORLD
CHEESE FILLING

I developed this recipe while making a filling for cheese Danish. The resulting taste reminded me of my Rumanian grandmother's blintzes, thus the title in her honor.

4 ounces cream cheese, at
　　room temperature
1/2 pound baker's or farmer's
　　cheese, at room
　　temperature
1 egg yolk
1/3 cup honey
1 tablespoon flour
1/4 teaspoon ground
　　cinnamon
1/8 teaspoon ground cloves
1/8 teaspoon ground
　　nutmeg
1/4 cup *each* sultanas and
　　dark raisins, plumped in
　　2 tablespoons Cognac
Grated zest of 1 orange
1/4 teaspoon vanilla extract

Cream together the cream cheese and baker's or farmer's cheese. Add the egg yolk, honey and flour and beat until smooth. Add the spices, raisins, orange zest and vanilla extract and mix well.
Makes approximately 2 cups

POPPY-SEED FILLING

The basis for popular fillings in Germany, Russia and Slavic countries, poppy seeds lend a unique flavor and color to baked goods. This recipe is a wonderful filling for Hamantashen or other filled cookies. The addition of cream cheese or cottage cheese turns it into a filling for coffee cakes.

1/2 cup poppy seeds
1/4 cup milk or unsweetened
　　apple, grape or orange juice
1/3 cup honey
3 tablespoons butter
2 egg yolks
Grated zest of 1/2 lemon
1/4 teaspoon ground
　　cinnamon
1/2 teaspoon vanilla extract
1/2 cup ground lightly
　　toasted almonds
1/2 pound cream cheese or
　　cottage cheese, sieved
　　(optional)

Put the poppy seeds in a blender container and grind about 1 minute, or until they are coarsely ground. Transfer them to the top pan of a double boiler and add the milk or fruit juice. Place over gently boiling water until just heated through. Remove from the heat and stir in the honey, 2 tablespoons of the butter, the egg yolks, lemon zest and cinnamon. Return to the heat and cook over gently boiling water until quite thick, stirring occasionally. Remove from the heat and stir in the vanilla extract, almonds and the remaining 1 tablespoon butter.

For a coffee-cake filling, bring the cream cheese or sieved cottage cheese to room temperature and cream until smooth. Beat in the poppy-seed mixture and taste for flavoring. Adjust with more honey, cinnamon, vanilla extract and/or lemon zest, if necessary.
Makes approximately 1 cup without cheese, 2 cups with cheese.

SPICED RAISIN FILLING

Great for coffee cakes and cinnamon rolls, this filling can be used as is or beaten into cream cheese. And, if you have leftover cake or cookie crumbs, Streusel or Graham-Cracker Crust, one half to one cup added with the nuts would be a nice addition for both flavor and texture.

1 cup dark raisins
3/4 cup sultanas
3 tablespoons Cognac, rum, Grand Marnier or fresh orange juice
1/4 cup firmly packed brown sugar
Grated zest of 1 orange
3/4 teaspoon ground cinnamon
1/4 teaspoon ground cardamom
1 banana, mashed (optional)
1/2 cup lightly toasted walnuts, coarsely chopped
1 pound cream cheese, at room temperature (optional)

Combine all of the ingredients except the walnuts and cream cheese and mix well. Cover and refrigerate overnight to soften and flavor the raisins.

When ready to use, stir in the nuts if you are not using the cream cheese. If using the cream cheese, cream it until smooth, then beat in the raisin filling and taste for flavoring. Adjust with more sugar, orange zest, cinnamon and/or cardamom, if necessary, then stir in the nuts.
Makes approximately 3 cups without cream cheese,
5 cups with cream cheese

VARIATIONS Substitute chopped dried peaches, apricots or other fruit for part or all of the sultanas.

41

PRESERVES

Homemade preserves can add sparkle to your desserts. Folded into whipped cream, they make a delicious ribbon between cake layers. They can be melted and brushed over fresh fruit tarts for a beautiful glaze, spiraled in a jelly roll or mixed with cream cheese for coffee-cake fillings. Simply blended with yoghurt, they make a satisfying tea-time treat.

BASICS OF PRESERVING

EQUIPMENT You will need a large preserving kettle, preferably of heavy aluminum with a broad, flat bottom. A long-handled wooden spoon is good for stirring the preserves as they cook, and a long-handled slotted metal spoon with flat bowl is necessary for skimming any foam that forms on the surface of the boiling fruit. A wide-mouthed funnel and a ladle simplify transferring the hot preserves from the kettle to the jars. You will also need the standard-kitchen assortment of measuring cups and spoons, knives and bowls of various sizes. A jelly or deep-fat thermometer is a reliable test for the "jelly stage" (220° to 222°F), and household scales are handy for accurate measurement of fruit quantities.

JARS AND HOW TO STERILIZE THEM Mason, Kerr and Ball jars, available at hardware stores and some supermarkets, can be reused each year provided that new lids are used each time to ensure a good seal. Before using the jars, look them over carefully, making sure there are no nicks, cracks or other defects on the tops.

Wash the jars in hot, sudsy water and rinse them in scalding water. Place them in a

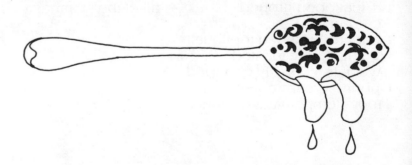

large kettle, along with the lids, cover with water and bring the water to a steady boil. Continue boiling for five minutes, turn off the heat and let the jars stand in the water until you are ready to use them. Then invert them onto a rack to dry, but fill them while they are still hot.

If paraffin rather than the two-part canning lid is used to seal the jar, select straight-sided ones. The straight sides make it easier to remove the paraffin. These jars should be sterilized in the same manner as the standard canning jars.

FILLING THE JARS Fill the sterilized jars to within one quarter inch of the top. This air space, called head room space, between the contents and the lid is necessary to create suction to ensure a perfect vacuum. Be sure to wipe the rim and threads of the jar tops with a hot damp cloth to remove any food traces, then screw on lids tightly.

SEALING WITH PARAFFIN Paraffin is available at most supermarkets. To use, fill jars, leaving one half-inch head room space. Wipe the top of the jar clean of any food traces. While the preserves are hot, top with a one eighth-inch layer of melted paraffin. When the paraffin has solidified, add another layer, rotating the jar to seal well.

STORAGE Twenty-four hours after filling and sealing your jars, check if the seals are good. Remove the rings and look for a slight depression in the lid tops. This means the seal is good. Or tap the lid with a spoon. It should emit a clear ringing sound. If the seal is not good, the preserves should be refrigerated and eaten right away, or you can empty the contents into a kettle, reheat and rejar. To store, label and date the jars and keep in a cool, dark place. The flavors will have mellowed after about two weeks.

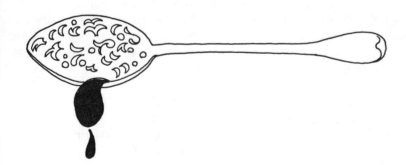

CANTALOUPE AND PEACH CONSERVE

4 cups peeled and sliced
  peaches
4 cups diced cantaloupe
2 lemons, unpeeled and
  thinly sliced
3 cups granulated white
  sugar
1 cup chopped walnuts

Combine the peaches, cantaloupe, lemons and sugar in a kettle. Cook over medium heat, stirring constantly, until sugar has dissolved. Bring to a boil and cook over high heat, stirring constantly, until a jelly thermometer registers 220° to 222°F, or the liquid sheets from a spoon (2 drops falling from side of spoon and forming 1 drop). This should take 30 to 40 minutes. Stir in walnuts and cook 2 minutes longer. Ladle into hot, sterilized jars and seal immediately.
*Makes approximately
6 half-pints*

CRANBERRY CONSERVE

3 oranges, unpeeled and
  thinly sliced
1 lemon, unpeeled and
  thinly sliced
1 pound cranberries
2-1/2 cups finely chopped
  fresh pineapple
1 cup raisins
1 cup dried currants
4 cups granulated white
  sugar, or 2 cups honey
1 cup unsweetened apple
  juice
1 cup chopped almonds

Combine the oranges, lemon, cranberries, pineapple, raisins, currants, sugar or honey and apple juice in a kettle. Cook over low heat, stirring constantly, until sugar has dissolved. Continue cooking over low heat until very thick, stirring occasionally, about 45 minutes. Stir in the almonds and cook 2 minutes longer. Ladle into hot, sterilized jars and seal immediately.
*Makes approximately
10 half-pints*

SANTA ROSA PLUM CONSERVE

2-1/2 quarts pitted and
  halved Santa Rosa plums
2 cups sliced peeled and
  pitted peaches
2 oranges, unpeeled and
  thinly sliced
1 lemon, unpeeled and thinly
  sliced
2 cups raisins
4 cups honey, or 8 cups
  granulated white sugar
1/2 pound chopped walnuts

Combine the plums, peaches, oranges, lemon, raisins and honey or sugar in a kettle. Cook over low heat, stirring constantly, until the sugar has dissolved. Raise heat and simmer, uncovered, stirring constantly, until a jelly thermometer registers 220° to 222°F, or the liquid sheets from a spoon (2 drops falling from side of spoon and forming 1 drop). This should take about 40 minutes. Ladle into hot, sterilized jars and seal immediately.
*Makes approximately
11 half-pints*

APPLE-BLUEBERRY CONSERVE

5 cups chopped cored and
  peeled tart apples
5 cups stemmed blueberries
1-1/2 cups honey
1/2 cup raisins
1/3 cup fresh lemon juice
1/2 cup chopped walnuts

Combine the apples, blueberries, honey, raisins and lemon juice in a kettle. Bring the mixture to a boil over medium heat, lower the heat and simmer, uncovered, stirring constantly, until the mixture thickens, about 45 minutes. Stir in the walnuts and cook about 2 minutes longer. Ladle into hot, sterilized jars and seal immediately.
*Makes approximately
6 half-pints*

BLUEBERRY JAM

When there are a lot of blueberries, too many to eat in one day, make jam.

Blueberries, in quantity
  desired
Honey or granulated white
  sugar

Wash and stem blueberries, measure and place in a kettle. Cook over low heat, stirring, until berries begin to give forth their juice. Add 1/4 cup honey *or* 1/2 cup sugar for each cup of fruit. Bring to a boil and cook over high heat until a jelly thermometer registers 220° to 222°F, or the liquid sheets from a spoon (2 drops falling from side of spoon and forming 1 drop). This should take about 30 minutes. Ladle into hot, sterilized jars and seal immediately.

45

PLUM JAM

3 quarts pitted and halved
   (or quartered if large) plums
1 cup unsweetened apple
   juice
2 cups honey
1-1/2 cups raisins
1 teaspoon ground
   cinnamon

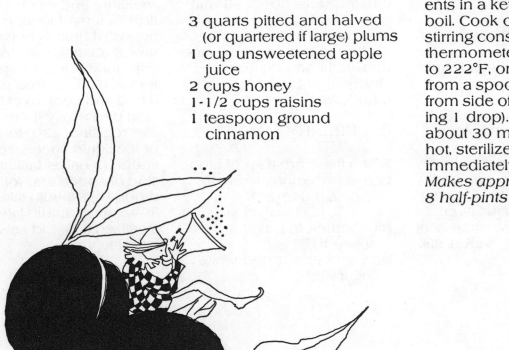

Combine all of the ingredients in a kettle and bring to a boil. Cook over high heat, stirring constantly, until a jelly thermometer registers 220° to 222°F, or the liquid sheets from a spoon (2 drops falling from side of spoon and forming 1 drop). This should take about 30 minutes. Ladle into hot, sterilized jars and seal immediately.
*Makes approximately
8 half-pints*

APRICOT OR PEACH PRESERVES

Peaches or apricots, in
   quantity desired
Granulated white sugar

Peel, pit and thickly slice
peaches or apricots. Mea-
sure and cover with 1/2 cup
sugar for each cup of fruit.
Let stand 12 hours or overnight. Transfer to a kettle and
place over medium heat, stirring constantly, until sugar
has dissolved. Bring to a boil
and cook over high heat, stirring constantly, 30 to 35
minutes. Ladle into hot, sterilized jars and seal imme-
diately.

APRICOT-PEACH PRESERVES Use
half peaches and half apricots. Proceed as directed
above.

QUINCE-ORANGE PRESERVES

These preserves are a beautiful peach color. Fold into
whipped cream and spread
between the layers of a carrot
cake.

6 or 7 quince (approximately
   2 pounds peeled and
   cored)
1/2 pound seedless oranges,
   unpeeled
One 6-ounce can frozen
   orange juice concentrate,
   thawed and diluted with
   fresh lemon juice to
   measure 2 cups
1-1/4 cups granulated white
   sugar

Peel and core the quince. As
you finish each one, drop it
into a bowl containing the
orange-lemon juice mixture.
(This will prevent the quince
from discoloring.) Coarsely
grate the quinces and oranges.
Combine with the orange-
lemon juice mixture and
sugar in a kettle. Cook over
low heat, stirring constantly,
until the sugar has dissolved.
Bring to a boil and cook over
high heat, stirring constantly,
until a jelly thermometer registers 220° to 222°F, or the
liquid sheets from a spoon
(2 drops falling from side of
spoon and forming 1 drop).
Ladle into hot, sterilized jars
and seal immediately.
*Makes approximately
6 half-pints*

AMBER MARMALADE

A favorite of mine, this marmalade is wonderfully bitter. If you wish a sweeter result, use the larger amount of sugar indicated.

1 grapefruit
1 orange
1 lemon
3 quarts water
6 or 8 cups granulated white sugar

Thinly slice the unpeeled fruit, cover with the water and let stand overnight. The next morning, place the fruit and water in a kettle and simmer, uncovered, over low heat until the fruit is tender, about 45 minutes to 1 hour. Remove from the heat and let stand 6 hours. Return to the heat, add the sugar and cook over medium heat, stirring constantly, until sugar has dissolved. Then cook over high heat until a jelly thermometer registers 220° to 222°F, or the liquid sheets from a spoon (2 drops falling from side of spoon and forming 1 drop). Ladle into hot, sterilized jars and seal immediately.
Makes approximately
6 half-pints

TOASTED NUTS

It is a good idea to toast any nuts you are going to use as it intensifies their flavor.

Spread whole or sliced nuts on a baking sheet and place in a preheated 375°F oven for about 10 minutes, shaking the pan once or twice to prevent the nuts from burning. Remove from the oven when lightly golden and let cool. Leave whole or chop or grind to the desired consistency.

PRALINE

Crush and then pat against the sides of a cake for lovely texture and flavor, or use as a garnish for mousse.

1 cup granulated white
   sugar
1/2 cup water
1 cup toasted sliced almonds

Combine the sugar and water in a heavy-bottomed saucepan and cook over low heat, stirring, until the sugar has dissolved. Raise the heat and cook until a nice caramel color is reached. Do not stir the mixture, but periodically brush down any sugar crystals clinging to the sides of the pan with a natural bristle brush dipped in cold water. Add the almonds and stir with a wooden spoon until they are well coated. Immediately pour onto a well-oiled baking sheet in a thin layer and allow to cool completely. Break into fine pieces (a blender works well) and store in an airtight container in a cool, dry place.
Makes approximately 1 cup

NEEDLETHREADS

Also called julienned orange and lemon peel, these lovely slips of color are perfect for garnishing any citrus-based dessert: Lemon Mousse, Gâteau au Citron, Lemon-Walnut Roll.

1 orange
1 lemon
1 cup water

With a vegetable peeler or utensil specifically designed for the purpose, peel the colored portion only of the rind from each fruit. With a sharp knife, cut the rind lengthwise into *very thin* strips, about 1/64 inch wide. Bring the water to a boil in a small saucepan and add the citrus strips. Boil for 1 minute then pour through a strainer. Set the strips out to dry completely before using.

STRAWBERRY-ALMOND DAISIES

I first thought of using strawberries and almonds in this combination while creating Gâteau Belle Hélène. The daisies would also be pretty garnishing a savarin or babas, or perhaps the top of a strawberry mousse.

Whole strawberries
Toasted sliced almonds

Slice off thin rounds of skin from the strawberries for the centers of the daisies and surround with "petals" of sliced almonds, trying to use the same-size almond slice for each petal.

Masterpieces

Celebration

All of these recipes are very special. They use the purest flavorings, sweetest creams, the most flavorful fruits and fillings. All are masterpieces.

ALMOND CAKE

I was first shown this recipe while working at a northern Italian restaurant in Portland, Oregon. When I left there, I despaired of ever finding the recipe again. Then one day while looking through a cookbook ... a few changes, like substituting almond paste for ground almonds, and the original almond cake was "recreated." Narsai David suggests a topping of raspberry purée for an even more perfect blending of flavors.

1/4 pound unsalted butter, at room temperature
3/4 cup granulated white sugar
1 cup almond paste
3 eggs
1/3 teaspoon baking powder
Pinch of salt
1/4 teaspoon almond extract
1 tablespoon Kirsch or Grand Marnier
1/4 cup *sifted* cake flour
Confectioners' sugar

Line an 8-inch round pan with parchment paper or butter and flour. Preheat the oven to 350°F.

Cream together the butter and sugar until light and fluffy. Add the almond paste and beat in well. Beat in the eggs, one at a time. Add the baking powder, salt, almond extract and Kirsch or Grand Marnier and mix in well. Fold in the flour, being careful not to overmix the batter (use the lowest speed on your mixer). Transfer the batter to the prepared cake pan, mounding the center slightly higher than the sides.

Place in the preheated oven and bake about 40 minutes, or until golden brown and a toothpick inserted in the center comes forth clean. Let cool slightly on a wire rack, then turn out of the pan onto the rack. When completely cool, dust with confectioners' sugar. *Makes one 8-inch cake*

BANANA CAKE

There are many ways to decorate this cake. It can be topped with apricot jam and Chocolate Glaze, whipped cream, Chocolate Mousse, Chocolate Butter Cream, Cream-Cheese Frosting or confectioners' sugar, and filled with whipped cream, chocolate mousse or whipped cream and strawberries. Garnish with chocolate curls, ground toasted nuts, or strawberries to match a strawberry and cream filling. This cake may be baked in round pans or in a sheet pan to form a square or rectangular cake.

1/4 pound butter
3/4 cup firmly packed
    brown sugar
3/4 cup granulated white
    sugar
2 eggs
1/2 teaspoon baking powder
3/4 teaspoon baking soda
1/2 teaspoon salt
1 cup mashed bananas
    (approximately 2 bananas)
1 teaspoon vanilla extract
1/4 cup plain yoghurt, sour
    cream or buttermilk
1-1/4 cups all-purpose or
    unbleached white flour or
    half whole-wheat flour
    and half white flour
1 cup finely ground lightly
    toasted walnuts, hazelnuts
    or almonds

Line with parchment paper or butter and flour three 8-inch or two 9-inch pans or one 11- by 16-inch pan. Preheat the oven to 350°F.

Cream together the butter and sugars. Add the eggs, one at a time, beating in well. Mix in the baking powder, baking soda and salt. Mix the mashed bananas with the vanilla extract and yoghurt, sour cream or buttermilk. Stir the flour into the butter-egg mixture, then mix in the bananas and nuts. Pour the batter into the prepared pan(s) and bake in the preheated oven about 20 minutes for the small pans and 30 minutes for the large one, or until a toothpick inserted in the center comes forth clean. Let cool slightly on wire rack(s), then turn out of the pan(s) onto the rack(s) to cool completely.

*Makes three 8-inch layers,
two 9-inch layers or
one 11- by 16-inch sheet
cake*

CRANBERRY UPSIDE-DOWN CAKE

A beautiful alternative to pineapple.

4 tablespoons butter
2/3 cup plus 2 tablespoons honey
2 tablespoons freshly grated orange zest
1-1/2 teaspoons vanilla extract
1-1/2 cups fresh cranberries
1 cup chopped lightly toasted walnuts
2 tablespoons fresh orange juice
1/4 cup safflower or sunflower oil
1 egg
1 teaspoon baking soda
1/4 teaspoon salt
1 cup all-purpose or unbleached white or whole-wheat flour
1/2 cup plain yoghurt or buttermilk

Line an 8-inch-square pan with parchment paper or butter and flour. Preheat the oven to 350°F.

Cream together the butter and 1/3 cup of the honey. Blend in 1 tablespoon of the orange zest and 1/2 teaspoon of the vanilla extract. Spread in the bottom of the prepared pan. Mix the whole cranberries and nuts with 2 tablespoons of the honey and the orange juice. Spread over the mixture in the pan.

Mix together the remaining 1/3 cup honey and the oil.

Add the egg and beat well. Mix in the remaining 1 tablespoon orange zest, the vanilla, baking soda and salt. Stir in the flour and the yoghurt or buttermilk. Pour this mixture over the cranberries in the pan and bake in the preheated oven for about 30 minutes, or until a toothpick inserted in the center comes forth clean. Remove from the oven and invert onto a serving plate immediately. Peel off parchment, if used, and serve warm or cold.

Makes one 8-inch cake

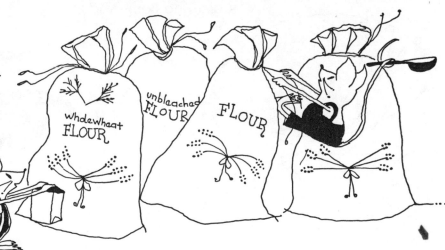

53

LEMON PUDDING CAKE

When I was growing up, my mother made pudding cake from a mix. What a wonderful surprise to taste the real thing at a dinner party one evening in Gualala. The hostess, Dorothy Reuf, set the cake in the riverbed to chill. Dorothy's recipe comes from South Africa, where her mother needed a way to "use the lemons from the great lemon trees they had there." Dorothy uses a soufflé dish for a lot of "puddingness"; her mother uses a rectangular dish for less.

3 tablespoons butter
1/3 cup granulated white
  sugar
1/4 cup all-purpose or
  unbleached white or
  whole-wheat flour
3 egg yolks
2 teaspoons freshly grated
  lemon zest
1/4 cup fresh lemon juice
1-1/2 cups milk
3 egg whites
1/4 teaspoon salt
Additional 1/4 cup sugar

Butter a 1-quart soufflé dish or a 7- by 10-inch baking dish. Preheat the oven to 325°F.

Cream together the butter, sugar and flour. Add the egg yolks, one at a time. Stir in the lemon zest and juice and the milk. Set aside.

Beat the egg whites until soft peaks form, add the salt, then gradually beat in 1/4 cup sugar until stiff peaks form. Fold the butter-lemon mixture into the whites until no white streaks show. Pour the batter into the prepared dish and set in a pan with water to a depth of 1 inch. Bake in the preheated oven for 1 hour. Serve from the pan. This cake tastes best warm, though it is also good chilled.
Makes 8 servings

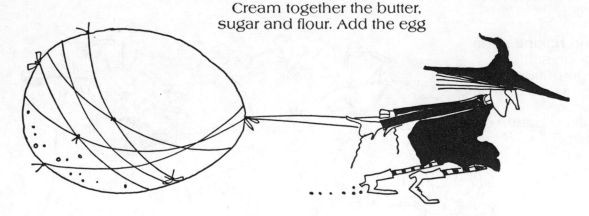

54

CARROT CAKE

One of my favorite cakes. This recipe produces a particularly moist, flavorful, nicely textured result. The first wedding cake I created was a carrot cake. That time I used ground pine nuts and they imparted a wonderful flavor. Once in Canada at a "health retreat" I made this cake using ground sunflower and sesame seeds, which also was a success. You may mask this cake with flavored whipped cream or Cream-Cheese Frosting or dust it with confectioners' sugar.

5 ounces safflower or
 sunflower oil*
1/2 cup *each* firmly packed
 brown sugar and granu-
 lated white sugar, or
 1/2 cup honey
3 eggs
1 teaspoon baking powder
1 teaspoon baking soda
1/2 teaspoon salt
1 teaspoon ground
 cinnamon
1/2 cup unbleached or all-
 purpose white or whole-
 wheat flour
2-1/2 cups grated carrots
 (approximately 4 to 6 medium carrots)
1/4 cup raisins, plumped
1/2 cup ground lightly
 toasted walnuts or nuts or
 seeds of choice

Line an 8-inch round pan with parchment paper or butter and flour. Preheat the oven to 350°F.

With an electric mixer, beat together the oil and sugars or honey. Add the eggs, one at a time, beating well after each addition. Mix in the baking powder, baking soda, salt and cinnamon. Lower the speed and add the flour, carrots, raisins and nuts. Pour the batter into the prepared pan and bake in the preheated oven for about 35 to 45 minutes, or until a toothpick inserted in the center comes forth clean. Let cool slightly on a wire rack, then turn out of the pan onto the rack to cool completely before splitting and icing.
Makes one 8-inch cake

*If using honey for sweetening, reduce the oil measure to 1/2 cup.

CHOCOLATE CAKE NEWPORT BEACH

This cake received its name in fond memory of my days at the TeenAge Fair in Hollywood, where I had my first chocolate-coated frozen banana. That memory made me think of my teenage days at the ocean.

1 recipe Chocolate Génoise (two 8-inch cakes), page 21
1/2 cup Spiced Orange Syrup, page 36
1-1/3 cups heavy cream
3 tablespoons confectioners' sugar
2 ripe bananas, thinly sliced

1/4 cup Apricot Glaze, flavored with brandy, page 27, heated
1/2 recipe Chocolate Glaze, page 29, heated
3/4 cup chopped lightly toasted walnuts

56

Split each cake in half horizontally to form 4 layers. Lace each layer with some of the orange syrup. Whip the cream with the confectioners' sugar and sandwich the layers together with about a 1/4-inch thickness of cream topped with the sliced bananas, reserving the remaining cream for use later. Drizzle the top layer with the hot Apricot Glaze, let cool, then cover with the hot Chocolate Glaze. Place the cake in the refrigerator to chill for 30 minutes.

When the cake is chilled, mask the sides with some of the remaining whipped cream and pat the chopped walnuts onto it. With a pastry bag fitted with a small plain tip, write "Newport Beach" in fanciful script on top of the cake with some of the remaining cream. Replace the tip with a large star tip and pipe rosettes around the top edge of the cake with the remaining whipped cream.
Makes 12 servings

ORANGE-CRANBERRY CAKE

Plan to make this cake a day in advance of serving so that the flavors blend completely.

2-1/4 cups *sifted* unbleached or all-purpose white flour
1 cup granulated white sugar
1/4 teaspoon salt
1 teaspoon baking powder
1 teaspoon baking soda
1 cup chopped lightly toasted walnuts
1 cup raisins
1 cup cranberries
Grated zest of 2 oranges
2 eggs, beaten
1 cup sour cream or plain yoghurt
3/4 cup safflower or sunflower oil
1 cup heavy cream, whipped with orange-flavored liqueur to taste

Basting syrup
1 cup granulated white sugar
1 cup frozen orange juice concentrate, thawed

Butter a 10-inch tube pan. Preheat the oven to 350°F.

Sift together the sifted flour, sugar, salt, baking powder and baking soda. Stir in the nuts, raisins, cranberries and orange zest. Mix together the eggs, sour cream or yoghurt and oil and stir into the flour mixture. Pour the batter into the prepared pan and bake in the preheated oven for about 1 hour, or until a toothpick inserted in the center comes forth clean. Cool on a wire rack for 15 minutes before removing from the pan to a serving plate.

Prepare the basting syrup by combining the orange juice concentrate and sugar in a saucepan. Heat to boiling, stirring to dissolve the sugar. Prick the cake all over with the tines of a fork. While the syrup is hot, pour it over the cake. Baste with the drippings until they are all absorbed. Refrigerate at least 24 hours, then serve with whipped cream piled in the center.
Makes 10 to 12 servings

CHOCOLATE DECADENCE

The original, most sinful chocolate dessert. I developed this recipe when I was a pastry chef at Narsai's restaurant in Berkeley. A friend asked for something both very chocolate and very decadent for his dinner guest (thereby unintentionally naming the dessert). They were overwhelmed, as have been all chocolate aficionados who have since tasted this confection. Narsai added the raspberry purée to complete the development of Chocolate Decadence.

1 pound semisweet chocolate
1/4 pound plus 2 tablespoons butter
5 eggs
1 tablespoon granulated white sugar
1 tablespoon all-purpose or unbleached white flour
2 cups heavy cream
1/4 cup confectioners' sugar
1 tablespoon Grand Marnier
1 teaspoon vanilla extract
4 ounces semisweet chocolate, slightly warmed
12 ounces frozen raspberries, thawed, puréed and strained

Line an 8-inch round cake pan with parchment paper or butter and flour. Preheat the oven to 425°F.

Combine the 1 pound semisweet chocolate and butter in the top pan of a double boiler placed over simmering water and heat just until melted; set aside. Combine the eggs and sugar in the top pan of a double boiler placed over simmering water and, with a wire whisk, whip just until warm to the touch. Immediately remove the egg-sugar mixture to a mixing bowl and whip at the highest speed of your electric mixer until tripled in bulk and very light.

Using your hand or a wire whisk, fold the flour and the chocolate mixture into the eggs, being careful not to deflate the eggs but folding thoroughly. Pour this mixture into the prepared pan and bounce the pan once on the counter top to remove all the air bubbles.

Bake in the preheated oven for 15 minutes. Remove from the oven (the cake should still be soft in the center) and let cool to room temperature. Wrap and freeze for at least 12 hours, or up to 1 month.

To unmold, spin the pan for 15 seconds over a lit gas burner or electric range burner preheated on medium heat, then invert onto a plate.

Whip the cream until soft peaks form, add the confec- tioners' sugar, Grand Marnier and vanilla extract and whip until stiff peaks form. *Do not overbeat.* Mask the entire decadence with the cream, reserving some for piping a circle of rosettes around the outside of the top edge. With a vegetable peeler, make chocolate curls from the warmed chocolate and fill the center of the decadence with them.

Allow the cake to set out for 30 minutes before serving to permit the maximum taste experience. To serve, spoon a pool of raspberry purée on each individual's plate, or spoon the purée over the top of each serving. *Makes 12 servings*

GATEAU AU CITRON

Lemon cake at its best. The addition of the praline on the sides gives a wonderful texture to each mouthful.

1 recipe Génoise (two 8-inch cakes), page 20-21
1/2 to 3/4 cup Spiced Orange Syrup, page 36
1 recipe Lemon Filling, page 39
1 cup heavy cream
1 teaspoon vanilla extract
3 tablespoons confectioners' sugar
1 cup crushed Praline, page 49
Needlethreads of orange and lemon, page 49

Split each cake horizontally into as many layers as desired. Lace each layer with some of the orange syrup. Sandwich the layers together with a thin coating of the lemon filling. Spread a thin layer of lemon filling on top of the cake as well.

Whip the cream with the vanilla extract and confectioners' sugar and use a portion of it to mask the sides of the cake. Press the Praline onto the sides. With a pastry bag fitted with a large star tip, pipe rosettes around the top edge of the cake with the remaining cream. Garnish each rosette with the needlethreads.
Makes 12 servings

GATEAU SABRA

This cake is named after the Israeli liqueur, Sabra, a blend of chocolate and orange.

1 recipe Chocolate Génoise
   (two 8-inch rounds),
   page 21
1/2 to 3/4 cup Spiced
   Orange Syrup, page 36
Spiced Oranges using 3
   oranges, page 111, divided
   into segments
3 cups Chocolate Mousse,
   page 100
1-1/2 cups crushed Praline,
   page 49
2 ounces semisweet choco-
   late, slightly warmed

Split each cake in half horizontally to form 4 layers. Lace each layer with some of the orange syrup, including the top one. Sandwich the layers together with about a 1/4-inch thickness of the mousse and the orange segments. Mask the entire cake with some of the remaining mousse and press the Praline onto the sides. With a vegetable peeler, make chocolate curls from the chocolate by scraping it along its length. Mound the curls in the center of the cake. With a pastry bag fitted with a large star tip, pipe rosettes around the top edge of the cake.
Makes 12 servings

GATEAU MOCHA

Mocha is my favorite flavor. Here is a special cake for those who agree with me.

1 recipe Chocolate Génoise
   or plain Génoise flavored
   with vanilla extract *and*
   Cognac (two 8-inch cakes),
   page 20-21
1/3 cup Cognac, or
   1/2 to 3/4 cup Spiced
   Orange Syrup, page 36
1 recipe Mocha Butter
   Cream, page 31
1/4 cup Apricot Glaze, flavored with Cognac, page
   27, heated
1/2 recipe Chocolate Glaze,
   page 29, heated
1-1/2 cups finely chopped
   lightly toasted walnuts

Split each cake in half horizontally to form 4 layers. Lace each layer with some of the Cognac or orange syrup. Sandwich the layers together with about a 1/4-inch thickness of the butter cream. Drizzle the top layer with the hot Apricot Glaze, let cool, then cover with the hot Chocolate Glaze. Place the cake in the refrigerator to chill for 30 minutes.

When the cake is chilled, mask the sides with some of the remaining butter cream and press the walnuts onto the sides. With a pastry bag fitted with a large star tip, pipe rosettes around the top edge of the cake with the remaining butter cream.
Makes 12 servings

GATEAU MONTMORENCY

Here is my version of a Black Forest torte. The recipe calls for canned cherries, but use fresh dark cherries when they are in season, substituting Kirsch or Cognac for the can juice.

One 16-ounce can pitted
    dark sweet cherries, or
    2 cups pitted fresh dark
    cherries, halved
1 recipe Chocolate Génoise
    (two 8-inch cakes), page 21
1/3 cup Kirsch or Cognac, if
    using fresh cherries
1 recipe Chocolate-Cream
    Cheese Frosting, page 30,
    or Chocolate Mousse,
    page 100
1-1/2 cups lightly toasted
    sliced almonds

Drain the canned cherries, if using, reserving the juice. Cut the cherries in half and set aside. Split each of the cakes in half horizontally to form 4 layers. Lace each layer, including the top one, with some of the can juice or with Kirsch or Cognac if using fresh cherries. Sandwich the layers together with about a 1/4-inch thickness of the frosting or mousse and some of the cherries. Mask the entire cake with some of the remaining frosting or mousse and press the almonds onto the sides. With a pastry bag fitted with a large star tip, pipe rosettes around the top edge of the cake with the re-

maining frosting or mousse. Arrange the remaining halved cherries in a decorative pattern in the center.
Makes 12 servings

VARIATIONS Substitute 1 cup heavy cream, whipped and flavored with Kirsch or Cognac and confectioners' sugar, for the Chocolate-Cream Cheese Frosting or the Chocolate Mousse.

Chocolate curls can be combined with the cherries on top or used in place of them. To make, bring a piece of semisweet chocolate to slightly warmer than room temperature and, with a vegetable peeler, scrape along its length to form curls.

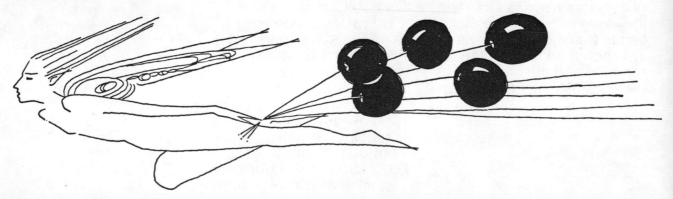

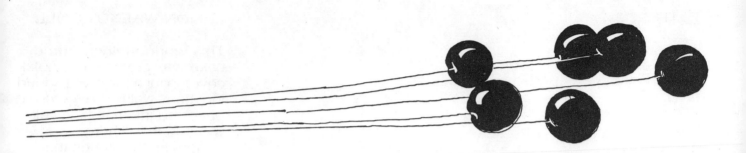

GATEAU BELLE HELENE

While at Narsai's, I created this cake one evening for Narsai's dinner guest, Madame Hélène Gravelin. Madame Gravelin was eight years old when her grandfather, Georges Auguste Escoffier, invented the celebrated combination of poached pears, vanilla ice cream and chocolate sauce in her honor.

1 recipe Génoise
  (two 8-inch cakes),
  page 20-21
1/2 to 3/4 cup Spiced
  Orange Syrup, page 36
1 basket strawberries
2 to 3 cups Chocolate
  Mousse, page 100
1 cup heavy cream

2 tablespoons Grand
  Marnier
1 teaspoon vanilla extract
1 cup lightly toasted sliced
  almonds
Strawberry-Almond Daisies,
  page 49

Split each cake in half horizontally to form 4 layers. Lace each layer with some of the orange syrup, including the top one. Hull the strawberries, reserve 2 large ones or 3 small ones for the Strawberry-Almond Daisies and slice the remainder. Sandwich the layers together with about a 1/4-inch thickness of the mousse and the sliced strawberries. Cover the syruplaced top with the remaining mousse. Whip the cream with the Grand Marnier and vanilla

extract and use a portion of it to mask the sides of the cake. Press the sliced almonds onto the sides, reserving some to make the daisies. Make Strawberry-Almond Daisies on the top of the mousse with the reserved whole strawberries and sliced almonds. With a pastry bag fitted with a large star tip, pipe rosettes around the top edge of the cake with the remaining whipped cream. *Makes 12 servings*

NOTE If desired, you may pipe rosettes of mousse rather than whipped cream around the top edge of the cake. You will need to prepare the larger quantity of mousse if you wish to do this.

LEMON-WALNUT ROLL

This wonderfully textured cake was created as a quick coverup for a mistake. I added too many walnuts to a *génoise* batter, so the resulting cake was too thin. There were visitors in the kitchen that day watching my moves, so I worked fast and rolled the *génoise* around a whipped-cream filling. It was my good fortune that they left impressed. Even better is this version, rolled around a lemon-cream filling.

1 recipe Génoise batter (11- by 16-inch jelly-roll pan), page 20-21, substituting 1/2 cup ground toasted walnuts for 1/2 cup of the flour and 1 tablespoon lemon juice and grated lemon zest from 1/2 lemon for the vanilla extract
1-1/4 cups heavy cream
1-1/2 tablespoons confectioners' sugar
1/2 tablespoon orange-flavored liqueur
1 recipe Lemon Filling, page 39
Granulated white sugar
1 recipe Apricot Glaze, flavored with 2 to 4 tablespoons orange-flavored liqueur, page 27, heated
8 to 12 toasted walnut halves

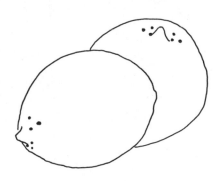

Line an 11- by 16-inch jelly-roll pan with parchment. Preheat the oven to 375°F. Prepare the cake batter, making the substitutions specified, and pour into the prepared pan. Bake in the preheated oven about 12 minutes, or until the cake's edges pull away from the sides of the pan and the top is golden. Remove from the oven and let cool on a wire rack to lukewarm.

Whip the cream until soft peaks form, then add the confectioners' sugar and orange-flavored liqueur and beat until stiff peaks form. Fold two thirds of the whipped cream into the lemon filling and set aside with the remaining cream.

Sprinkle granulated white sugar over a sheet of parchment about 1 inch larger in dimension than the jelly-roll pan. When the cake is luke-warm, loosen the edges with the point of a sharp knife, if necessary, and invert onto the sugared parchment, peeling off the parchment lining. Spread the lemon-whipped cream filling over the surface of the cake and, lifting the parchment from a long end, roll the cake inward jelly-roll fashion, being careful to keep the roll an even diameter throughout its length. Do not worry about any cracks that may form, as they can be obscured when the roll is decorated. Place the roll seam side down onto a serving platter. Paint entirely with the hot Apricot Glaze. With a pastry bag fitted with a small- or medium-sized star tip, pipe rosettes or shapes of choice onto the roll with the remaining whipped cream. Decorate with the walnut halves.
Makes 12 servings

DOUBLE CHOCOLATE ROLL

1 recipe Chocolate Cake for
    Rolling, page 22-23
Granulated white sugar
3 to 4 cups Chocolate
    Mousse, page 100

Prepare the cake according
to the recipe and let cool to
lukewarm. Sprinkle granu-
lated white sugar over a
sheet of parchment about 1
inch larger in dimension than
the jelly-roll pan. Loosen the
edges of the lukewarm cake
with the point of a sharp
knife, if necessary, and invert
onto the sugared parchment,
peeling off the parchment
lining. Spread about 3 cups
of the mousse in a thin layer
over the surface of the cake
and, lifting the parchment
from a long end, roll the cake
inward jelly-roll fashion. Do
not worry about any cracks
that may form, as they can
be obscured when the roll is
decorated. Place the roll seam
side down onto a serving
platter and chill thoroughly.
With a pastry bag fitted with
a small-sized star tip, pipe
decorative shapes onto the
roll with any remaining
mousse.
Makes 12 servings

VARIATION Whole or sliced
strawberries or other fruits
may also be used to deco-
rate this cake.

CHOCOLATE CREAM ROLL

1 recipe Chocolate Cake for
    Rolling, page 22-23
Granulated white sugar
1-1/2 cups heavy cream
1 tablespoon vanilla extract
    or liqueur of choice
1/4 cup confectioners' sugar

Prepare the cake according
to the recipe and let cool to
lukewarm. Sprinkle granu-
lated white sugar over a
sheet of parchment about 1
inch larger in dimension than
the jelly-roll pan. Loosen the
edges of the lukewarm cake
with the point of a sharp
knife, if necessary, and invert
onto the sugared parchment,

peeling off the parchment lining. Whip the cream until soft peaks form, then add the vanilla extract or liqueur and confectioners' sugar and beat until stiff peaks form. Spread a thin layer of the whipped cream over the surface of the cake and, lifting the parchment from a long end, roll the cake inward jelly-roll fashion. Do not worry about any cracks that may form, as they can be obscured when the roll is decorated. Place the roll seam side down onto a serving platter and chill thoroughly.

With a pastry bag fitted with a small-sized star tip, pipe decorative shapes onto the roll with any remaining whipped cream.
Makes 12 servings

VARIATIONS Top the whipped-cream filling with sliced strawberries. Or substitute a thin layer of raspberry or apricot jam or orange marmalade for the whipped cream, or make a thin layer of the preserves and top with the cream.

KIRSCH TORTE

This torte combines the flavors of Kirsch and almonds, but you can substitute any pairing desired—Cognac and hazelnuts, rum and pine nuts, Grand Marnier and almonds. . . .

Two 9-inch rounds Meringue Japonaise made with almonds, page 25
1 recipe Meringue-base French Butter Cream, page 31
1 recipe Gênoise (one 9-inch cake), page 20-21
1/4 to 1/3 cup Kirsch
1-1/2 cups lightly toasted sliced almonds

Place a meringue round on a serving plate and spread with a 1/4-inch layer of butter cream. Place the cake on top, lace with the Kirsch and then spread with a 1/4-inch layer of butter cream. Set the second meringue on top and press the layers together gently. Trim off the uneven edges of the meringue layers and crush and reserve the meringue trimmings for decoration, if desired.

Mask the entire cake with some of remaining butter cream. Press the almond slices and the crushed meringue, if desired, onto the sides. With a pastry bag fitted with a large star tip, pipe rosettes around the top edge of the cake with the remaining butter cream. Refrigerate at least 2 hours. Serve at room temperature.
Makes 12 servings

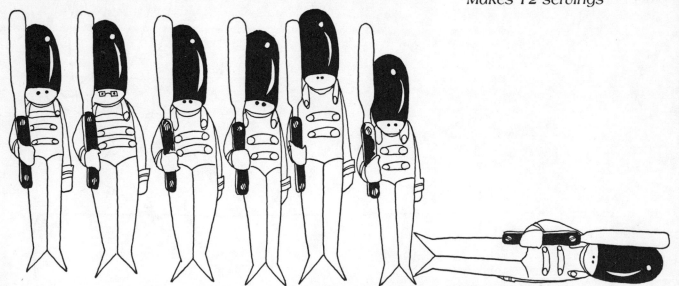

BUCHE DE NOEL

Inspired by the French custom of keeping a log burning throughout the Christmas supper, this traditional French yule log is quite beautiful when properly decorated with "stumps," "bark" and Meringue Mushrooms.

1 recipe Chocolate Cake for Rolling, page 22-23
Granulated white sugar
1 recipe Chocolate or Mocha Butter Cream, page 31
Meringue Mushrooms, page 121

Prepare the cake according to the recipe and let cool to lukewarm. Sprinkle granulated white sugar over a sheet of parchment about 1 inch larger in dimension than the jelly-roll pan. Loosen the edges of the lukewarm cake with the point of a sharp knife, if necessary, and invert onto the sugared parchment, peeling off the parchment lining. Spread a thin layer of some of the butter cream over the surface of the cake and, lifting the parchment from a long end, roll the cake inward jelly-roll fashion. Do not worry about any cracks that may form, as they can be obscured when the roll is decorated. Place the roll seam side down onto a serving platter and chill thoroughly before you begin decorating the "log."

Trim both ends of the roll at an angle and use the trimmings to form little "stumps" on the roll. With a pastry bag fitted with a small-sized star tip, pipe the remaining butter cream onto the roll simulating bark, forming knotholes where appropriate. (You may instead mask the entire roll with butter cream and use fork tines to form simulated bark.) Decorate the top with the mushrooms. *Makes 12 servings*

VARIATION The yule log may also be spread with a contrasting-flavored filling, such as rum-flavored pastry cream or chestnut-flavored butter cream.

SINFUL STRAWBERRIES

In Italian, this dessert is called *boccone dolce*—sweet mouthful. I was first shown a variation of this recipe while working as an instructor at a cooking school in Portland, Oregon. Chuck Miles, the founder of the school, told me the recipe was a classic at Sardi's in New York. Whether this is true or not, it can form the basis for classic desserts from your own kitchen. Substitute fruits, liqueurs or nuts as desired. Or even substitute indulgence for sanity as with the following recipe —bananas and peanut butter!

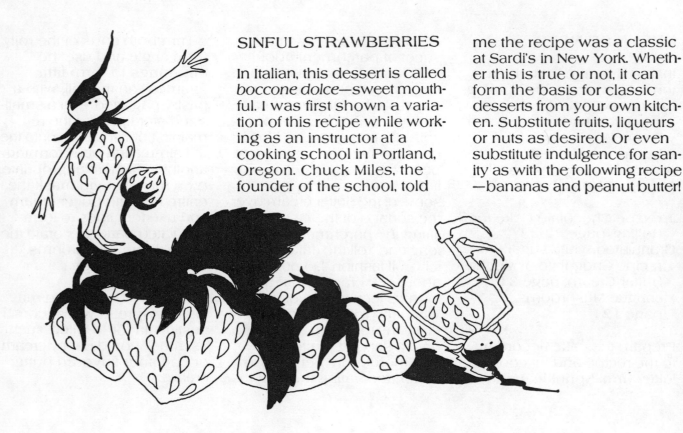

1 recipe Meringue Japonaise made with almonds, page 25
6 ounces semisweet chocolate
3 tablespoons orange-flavored liqueur
1/4 pound plus 4 tablespoons unsalted butter
2 baskets strawberries, hulled
2 cups heavy cream
1/4 cup confectioners' sugar
1 teaspoon vanilla extract
1 cup lightly toasted sliced almonds

Prepare the meringue mixture as directed in the recipe, piping it into 3 or 4 rounds. Bake as directed.

Combine the chocolate and liqueur in the top pan of a double boiler placed over simmering water and heat just until the chocolate melts. Remove from the heat and stir in the butter, a tablespoon at a time. Set aside.

Pick through the strawberries and select the 12 most perfect ones. Dip these 12 strawberries, one at a time, into the melted chocolate and place them on waxed paper to set. Slice the remaining strawberries and set aside.

Coat each of the meringue layers with an equal portion of the remaining chocolate. Whip the cream until soft peaks form, then add the confectioners' sugar and vanilla extract and beat until stiff peaks form. Sandwich together the chocolate-coated meringue layers with a filling of some of the whipped cream and the sliced strawberries, ending with a meringue layer. Trim off the uneven edges of the meringue layers. Mask the sides of the stacked meringues with whipped cream, reserving some for decoration, and press the sliced almonds onto the sides. Arrange the chocolate-dipped strawberries in the center on top. With a pastry bag fitted with a medium-sized star tip, pipe rosettes around the top edge with the remaining whipped cream. Refrigerate for at least 2 hours. Serve at room temperature.
Makes 10 servings

BAROQUE BANANAS

This is an unusual variation on Sinful Strawberries. While giving cooking demonstrations one fall, I had to create alternatives to out-of-season strawberries. Bananas came to mind, and with them "natural" substitutions like walnuts for the almonds, Cognac for the Grand Marnier and the addition of peanut butter to the chocolate. The top becomes wonderfully ridiculous, with chocolate-glazed banana tips forming a crown.

1 recipe Meringue Japonaise made with walnuts, page 25
8 ounces semisweet chocolate
1 cup smooth or crunchy peanut butter
1/2 cup Cognac
1/2 pound unsalted butter
3 teaspoons vanilla extract
5 or 6 ripe bananas
2 cups heavy cream
1/4 cup confectioners' sugar
Cognac as desired (optional)
1 cup ground lightly toasted walnuts

Prepare the meringue mixture as directed in the recipe, piping it into 3 rounds. Bake as directed.

Combine the chocolate, peanut butter and Cognac in the top pan of a double boiler placed over simmering water and heat just until the chocolate melts. Remove from the heat and stir in the butter, a tablespoon at a time. Then stir in 2 teaspoons of the vanilla extract.

Cut the ends off of each banana so that all of the tips are about 1 inch in length. Dip these tips, one at a time, into the melted chocolate and place them on waxed paper to set. Slice the remaining bananas about 1/8 inch thick.

Coat each of the meringue layers with an equal portion of the remaining chocolate. Whip the cream until soft peaks form, then add the confectioners' sugar, the remaining 1 teaspoon vanilla extract and Cognac to taste, if desired, and beat until stiff peaks form. Sandwich together the chocolate-coated meringue layers with a filling of some of the whipped cream and the sliced bananas, ending with a meringue layer. Trim off the uneven edges of the meringue layers, mask the sides of the stacked meringues with whipped cream, reserving some for decoration, and press the ground walnuts onto the sides. Arrange the chocolate-dipped banana tips in the center on top. With a pastry bag fitted with a medium-sized star tip, pipe rosettes around the top edge with the remaining whipped cream. Refrigerate at least 2 hours. Serve at room temperature.
Makes 10 servings

TORTE DE MILANO

This lovely torte was created in honor of Bruce and Theadora McBroom of the Old Milano Hotel in Gualala, California. The hotel was the site of many Sunday afternoon teas where several of the recipes in this book were lovingly tested and tasted.

1 recipe Meringue Japonaise, page 25
1 recipe Chocolate Butter Cream, page 31
1/4 cup Apricot Glaze, page 27, heated
1/2 recipe Chocolate Glaze, page 29, heated
1 cup lightly toasted sliced almonds

Prepare the meringue mixture as directed in the recipe, piping it into five 8-inch rounds. Bake as directed.

Sandwich together the meringue rounds with some of the butter cream, leaving the top round plain. Coat the top round with hot Apricot Glaze, let cool, then coat with the hot Chocolate Glaze.

Trim off the uneven edges of the meringue layers and crush and reserve the meringue trimmings for decoration, if desired. Mask the entire torte with some of the remaining butter cream and press the sliced almonds or a combination of almonds and the meringue trimmings onto the sides. With a pastry bag fitted with the smallest-sized plain tip, write Milano with butter cream on the cooled Chocolate Glaze. With a medium-sized star tip, pipe rosettes around the top edge of the torte with the remaining butter cream. Refrigerate at least 2 hours. Serve at room temperature.
Makes 10 servings

VIRTUOUS VANILLA

A lovely confection dedicated to the lighter side of decadence.

1 recipe Pastry Cream, page 38
1 recipe Chou Pastry dough, page 19
1/2 cup Apricot Glaze, flavored with 1 teaspoon fresh lemon juice, page 27, heated
1/2 cup lightly toasted sliced almonds
1 tablespoon unflavored gelatin, dissolved in 1/4 cup cold water
1 cup heavy cream
1/4 cup confectioners' sugar
1 teaspoon vanilla extract

Prepare the Pastry Cream and refrigerate it until you are ready to use it.

Preheat the oven to 375°F. Prepare the chou dough as directed in the recipe. Line a baking sheet with parchment paper or lightly butter and flour. With a pastry bag fitted with a large-sized plain tip, pipe the chou dough onto the parchment, forming a ring 9 inches in diameter, 2 inches wide and 1 inch high. Bake in the preheated oven for 35 minutes. Prick the pastry in 5 or 6 places and bake an additional 30 minutes.

With a knife with a serrated-edged blade, slice off the top third of the pastry in one piece to form a crown; set aside. With a spoon, scoop out any soft insides from the pastry bottom. Brush the hot Apricot Glaze on the inside bottom of the pastry ring and on the outside top of the crown. Immediately press the almonds onto the glazed portion of the crown.

Mix the gelatin-water mixture into the chilled Pastry Cream. Whip the heavy cream until soft peaks form, then add the confectioners' sugar and vanilla extract and beat until stiff peaks form. Fold the whipped cream, for no more than 5 seconds, into the Pastry Cream. Spoon this mixture into the cavity of the pastry bottom.

Put the crown in place on the pastry bottom. Refrigerate for at least 20 minutes before serving.
Makes 8 to 10 servings

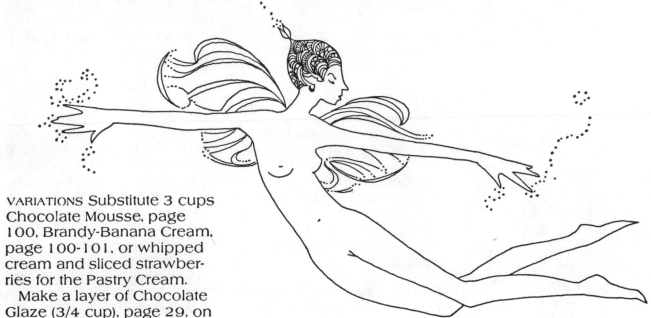

VARIATIONS Substitute 3 cups
Chocolate Mousse, page
100, Brandy-Banana Cream,
page 100-101, or whipped
cream and sliced strawberries for the Pastry Cream.

Make a layer of Chocolate
Glaze (3/4 cup), page 29, on
the crown, then top with the
Apricot Glaze and almonds.

Make a glaze with straw-
berry jelly, raspberry jam or
Amber Marmalade, page 48,
and use in place of the Apricot Glaze.

Substitute a liqueur of
choice for the vanilla extract
used to flavor the whipped
cream.

SAVARIN WITH ALMONDS
(Savarin d'Amandes)

Savarin, page 23, baked in a
   9-inch ring
1 cup granulated white
   sugar
1-1/2 cups water
1/2 cup Kirsch
1 tablespoon vanilla extract
1/2 cup Apricot Glaze,
   flavored with Kirsch,
   page 27, heated
1/2 cup lightly toasted sliced
   almonds
1 cup heavy cream
1/2 cup crushed Praline,
   page 49

Remove the savarin from the
oven and let cool to lukewarm. While it is cooling,
make a syrup by dissolving
the sugar in the water over
low heat, stirring constantly.
Bring to a boil and remove
from the heat. Stir in the
Kirsch and vanilla extract,
then cool to lukewarm.

When the savarin is luke-
warm, place it on a large
serving platter. Prick the top
and sides of the savarin with
the tines of a fork in several
places. Pour the lukewarm
Kirsch syrup over it and then
baste frequently for the next
30 minutes with any of the
syrup that has not been absorbed. Transfer the savarin
to a wire rack to drain, then
paint it with the hot Apricot
Glaze and sprinkle on the
almonds.

Whip the cream until stiff
peaks form. Fold the crushed
Praline into the cream and
mound the cream in the
center of the savarin. Serve
at room temperature.
Makes 8 to 10 servings

RUM BABAS
(Babas au Rhum)

1 recipe Savarin Dough,
    page 23, baked in 12 *baba*
    au rhum molds
1 cup granulated white
    sugar
1-1/2 cups water
1/2 cup dark rum
1 tablespoon vanilla extract
1/2 cup Apricot Glaze,
    flavored with dark rum,
    page 27, heated
Rum-flavored whipped
    cream

Remove the babas from the oven and let them cool to lukewarm. While they are cooling, make a syrup by dissolving the sugar in the water over low heat, stirring constantly. Bring to a boil and remove from the heat. Stir in the rum and vanilla extract, then cool to lukewarm.

When the babas are lukewarm, arrange them in a dish just large enough to hold them so that they are close together but not touching. Prick their tops with the tines of a fork in several places. Pour the lukewarm rum syrup over them and then baste frequently for the next 30 minutes with any of the syrup that has not been absorbed. Transfer the babas to a wire rack to drain, then paint them with the hot Apricot Glaze.

Serve the babas at room temperature with rum-flavored whipped cream.
Makes 12 servings

VARIATION Substitute a liqueur of choice for the rum and change the name of the recipe accordingly.

STEAMED PERSIMMON PUDDING

So that you may have persimmon pudding in May, freeze puréed persimmons in the winter in four-cup quantities. This recipe is from Barry Tasner, by way of Joyce Goldstein, by way of Paul Jacobs, by way of . . . with small changes along the way.

1 cup firmly packed brown sugar
1 cup granulated white sugar
1/4 pound plus 4 tablespoons butter, melted
2-1/2 cups *sifted* unbleached or all-purpose white flour
2-1/2 teaspoons ground cinnamon
3/4 teaspoon salt
4 cups persimmon purée
5 teaspoons baking soda, dissolved in
5 tablespoons hot water

5 tablespoons brandy
1-1/4 teaspoons vanilla extract
1-1/4 teaspoons fresh lemon juice
1/2 cup raisins
1/2 cup dried currants
3/4 cup chopped lightly toasted walnuts
5 eggs, lightly beaten
Hard Sauce, page 33

78

Add the sugars to the butter and mix well. Sift together the flour, cinnamon and salt. Stir into the butter-sugar mixture. Mix in the persimmon purée, baking soda-water mixture, brandy, vanilla extract, lemon juice, raisins, currants and nuts, then stir in the eggs. Transfer to 2 buttered 1-quart pudding molds with tubes and covers (or cover with cloths secured in place with string). Place the molds on racks set in the bottoms of 2 large pots and add water to reach two thirds of the way up the sides of the molds. Cover the pots with tightly fitting lids and steam in the gently boiling water for about 2-1/2 hours. Check the level of the water from time to time and add more if necessary to maintain the level. Serve, preferably warm, with Hard Sauce.
*Makes approximately
12 servings*

NARSAI DAVID'S PLUM PUDDING

The perfect dessert at holiday time.

1 cup firmly packed brown sugar
3 cups firmly packed cake crumbs
1/4 pound chopped beef suet
1 pound date paste or finely minced dates
1/3 cup applesauce
3 tablespoons brandy or rum
1 teaspoon ground cinnamon
1/4 teaspoon ground ginger
1/4 teaspoon ground mace
1/4 teaspoon ground cloves
1/4 teaspoon ground allspice
3/4 teaspoon salt
1/3 cup chopped lightly toasted walnuts or nuts of choice
1 cup dried currants
2/3 cup sultanas
2/3 cup dark raisins
3 ounces mixed candied citrus peel, chopped
1/2 lemon, ground with peel
1/2 orange, ground with peel
4 eggs, beaten
Narsai David's Cumberland Rum Butter, page 32, or Egg-Custard Sauce, page 33

Combine all of the ingredients, except the sauce, and mix well. Divide the mixture evenly among 3 buttered 1-quart pudding molds with tubes and covers (or cover with cloths secured in place with string). Place the molds on racks set in the bottoms of 3 large pots and add water to reach two thirds of the way up the sides of the molds. Cover the pots with tightly fitting lids and steam in gently boiling water for about 4 hours. Check the level of the water from time to time and add more if necessary to maintain the level. Serve, preferably warm, with Narsai David's Cumberland Rum Butter or Egg-Custard Sauce.
*Makes approximately
18 servings*

Queen of Tarts

Here are some of the masterpieces of the world of pies and tarts. They may all be served with pride, and with the knowledge that for most people (most Americans for sure), a piece of pie *is* dessert.

The major distinction between a pie and a tart is the shape. A pie is made in a round dish with slanted sides, while a tart has straight sides, is shallower (about three-fourths inch high) and is made in almost any shape: rectangular, square, oval, round. (You can create any shape you wish with aluminum foil. Just place a doubled, one-inch-high strip of it on a baking sheet in the shape you wish.)

Both pies and tarts are beautiful to behold, easy to prepare once you have mastered a couple of pastry recipes, and take good advantage of every fresh fruit as it comes into season.

ALMOND TART

I received this recipe from a friend in exchange for the one for Chocolate Decadence. It is a variation on the almond tart served at Berkeley's famous Chez Panisse restaurant. I have substituted my own basic pastry shell for the more temperamental one that came with the recipe.

1 cup lightly toasted
 sliced almonds
3/4 cup granulated white
 sugar
3/4 cup heavy cream
1 tablespoon Kirsch
1 tablespoon Grand Marnier
1/4 teaspoon almond
 extract
One 10-inch partially baked
 tart shell, page 15

Preheat the oven to 375°F. In a large mixing bowl, combine the almonds, sugar, cream, Kirsch, Grand Marnier and almond extract and mix well. Pour into the partially baked tart shell and bake in the preheated oven for 20 to 30 minutes, or until nicely browned on top.
Makes 8 to 10 servings

MALTED ALMOND TART

Here is a sugarless variation of the preceding Almond Tart.

1 egg
3/4 cup malt syrup
3/4 cup plain yoghurt
1 teaspoon vanilla extract
1 tablespoon Grand Marnier
1-1/2 cups lightly toasted
 sliced almonds
One 10-inch partially baked
 tart shell made with whole-
 wheat pastry flour,
 page 15

Preheat the oven to 375°F. Beat together the egg and the malt syrup. Beat in the yoghurt until the mixture is smooth. Add the vanilla extract, Grand Marnier and almonds and blend in well. Pour into the partially baked tart shell and bake in the preheated oven for 25 to 30 minutes, or until a caramel color on top.
Makes 8 to 10 servings

CRANBERRY TART

1 cup granulated white
  sugar
Grated zest and juice of
  1 orange
1 teaspoon ground
  cinnamon
4 cups (approximately
  1 pound) cranberries
1/2 teaspoon vanilla
  extract
1 recipe Almond-Cheese
  Filling, page 39
One 10-inch prebaked
  Sweet Pastry shell,
  page 17

Preheat the oven to 375°F.
Place the sugar in a heavy
saucepan. Measure the juice
from the orange and add
water to make 1 cup. Add
this juice mixture, the orange
zest and cinnamon to the
sugar. Bring to a boil over
low heat, stirring constantly.
Add the cranberries and cook
5 minutes, or until the cranberry skins pop. Remove
from the heat and let cool.
Stir in the vanilla extract.

Put the Almond-Cheese Filling in a layer in the bottom of
the tart shell. Place in the
preheated oven for 5 min-
utes. Remove from the oven
and let cool. Top the cooled
tart with the cooled cranberry mixture. Chill 30 minutes before serving.
Makes 8 to 10 servings

FRESH CHERRY TART

1/8 teaspoon ground
  cinnamon
1/8 teaspoon ground
  cardamom
3/4 cup ground lightly
  toasted walnuts or almonds
One 10-inch partially baked
  tart shell, page 15
1 pound dark cherries, pitted
1/2 cup granulated white
  sugar
1/2 cup Red Currant Jelly
  Glaze, page 27, heated

Preheat the oven to 350°F. Mix the cinnamon, cardamom and nuts together and sprinkle over the bottom of the partially baked tart shell. Toss the cherries with the sugar and arrange on top of the nuts in a single layer. Place on the lowest oven rack and bake for about 1 hour, or until the fruit's juices are bubbly. Remove from the oven and blush with the hot glaze.
Makes 8 to 10 servings

FRUIT TART OR PIE "AU NATUREL"

The unusual name of this tart comes from the fact that it contains no sugar, honey or other sweetener—just the natural sweetness of dates and coconut. This recipe was sent to me by my Canadian friend, Sharon Popowich. Sharon used fresh peaches in her pie. Apples were in season when I made it as a tart.

1-1/2 cups unsweetened shredded coconut
1 cup honey dates (or any sticky date), pitted and chopped
One 9- or 10-inch partially baked tart shell, page 15
4 or 5 apples or peaches, peeled and thinly sliced
1 cup plain yoghurt
1 teaspoon vanilla extract
2 eggs, beaten

Preheat the oven to 350°F. Mash together the coconut and dates until well blended and spread over the bottom of the partially baked shell. Arrange the apple or peach slices on top of the date-coconut mixture. Mix together the yoghurt, vanilla extract and eggs and pour over the fruit. Bake in the preheated oven about 25 minutes, or until the custard is set and the fruit is cooked. Serve warm or cold.
Makes 8 to 10 servings

NECTARINE, PEACH OR APRICOT TART

4 or 5 peaches or nectarines, peeled, pitted and sliced, or 8 or 9 apricots, peeled, pitted and halved
One 9-inch partially baked tart shell, page 15
1/4 cup granulated white sugar
2 tablespoons butter, cut into small bits
1/2 cup Apricot Glaze, page 27, heated

Preheat the oven to 350°F. Arrange the fruit in the tart shell. If using apricots, place them rounded side up in one layer. Sprinkle with the sugar and dot with the butter bits. Bake in the preheated oven for 30 to 45 minutes, or until the pie shell and the fruit are lightly browned. Remove from the oven and brush with the hot glaze.
Makes 8 servings

NOTE You may also use the pastry dough to line tartlet pans, in which case stand the slices on their sides, slightly overlapping one another to form a rose pattern. This will require about half again as much fruit, but the tarts look lovely. Give them a name to match their romantic look—Empassioned Peach Tartlets.

STRAWBERRY CREAM TART

One of my favorites. Especially nice as individual tartlets.

1 recipe Sweet Pastry dough, page 17
1 recipe Chocolate Glaze made with Semisweet Chocolate, flavored with Grand Marnier, page 29, heated
1 recipe Almond-Cheese Filling, page 39
1-1/2 baskets strawberries, hulled
1/2 cup strawberry jelly
1 to 2 tablespoons Grand Marnier or Kirsch
Confectioners' sugar

Preheat the oven to 375°F. Roll out the pastry dough and line a 10-inch tart pan or 5 individual tartlet pans. Prebake in the preheated oven as directed on page 18-19.

Brush the Chocolate Glaze onto the bottom(s) of the tart shell(s). Make a layer of the Almond-Cheese Filling on top of the chocolate lining. Arrange the strawberries, close together and pointed ends up, on top of the filling.

Melt the jelly in a small saucepan over medium heat and stir in the liqueur. When hot, brush the strawberry glaze over the berries. Refrigerate for no longer than 6 hours. Just before serving, dust the top with confectioners' sugar.
Makes 8 servings as a pie, 5 servings as tartlets

CINNAMON TART
(Tarte Cannelle)

1-1/2 recipes Sweet Pastry
   dough, sifting the flour with
   2 teaspoons ground
   cinnamon, page 17
3 cups stemmed blueberries
1/4 cup granulated white
   sugar
Confectioners' sugar

Make the pastry dough and
let it rest in the refrigerator
while preparing the blue-
berries.
   Combine the blueberries
and granulated sugar in a
heavy saucepan and stir over
low heat until the juices begin to run. Increase the heat
to medium and cook 10
minutes, stirring constantly.
Remove from the heat and
let cool to room temperature.
   Preheat the oven to 375°F.
Roll out two thirds of the
pastry and use it to line a 10-
inch tart pan. Fill the tart shell
with the cooled blueberries.
Roll out the remaining pastry
and cut into thin strips long
enough to reach the radius
of the tart pan. Arrange the
strips in a latticework pattern
over the fruit. Bake in the
preheated oven for about 25
minutes, or until the pastry is
crisp and lightly browned.
Remove from the oven and
let cool. Dust with confectioners' sugar just before serving.
Makes 8 servings

VARIATION Substitute apricots
for the blueberries and make
tartlets rather than a single
tart. Line 5 tartlet pans, using
all of the pastry. Peel and
slice the apricots and arrange
them in an attractive design
in the shells. Sprinkle lightly
with granulated white sugar
and dot each tartlet with 1
teaspoon butter, cut into bits.
Bake as directed above,
though just until the pastry is
lightly browned. Remove from
the oven and brush with 3/4
cup hot Apricot Glaze, page
27.

TARTE AUX POIRES
(Pear Tart)

Basically a pear tart, though I have included one quince and a few apples to improve the texture, flavor and color.

1 pound crisp apples
1 quince
3 pounds pears
1/3 cup Apricot Preserves, page 47
1 tablespoon vanilla extract or Cognac
2/3 cup granulated white sugar
3 tablespoons butter
3 ounces frozen orange juice concentrate, thawed

One 10-inch partially baked tart shell, page 15
1 cup Apricot Glaze,* page 27, heated

Peel, core and roughly chop the apples, quince and 2 pounds of the pears. Place in a heavy saucepan, cover and cook over low heat for about 20 minutes. When the fruit is tender, stir in the preserves, vanilla extract, sugar and butter. Remove from the heat and let cool.

Preheat the oven to 350°F. While the fruit is cooling, peel and slice the remaining pears and coat the slices with the orange juice concentrate.

Spread the cooked fruit over the bottom of the partially baked shell and neatly arrange the orange juice-coated pear slices on top, closely overlapping them. Bake the tart in the preheated oven for 30 to 45 minutes, or until lightly browned. Remove the tart from the oven and brush the top with the hot Apricot Glaze while still warm.
Makes 8 servings

*If you have flavored the cooked fruit with Cognac, add Cognac to taste to the Apricot Glaze.

TARTE DES DEMOISELLES TATIN

The story of the origin of this tart is wonderful: The Tatin sisters were proprietors of a country inn known throughout France for its excellent fare. Dessert one evening was to be a warm apple tart. As one of the sisters was bringing the tart from the kitchen to the awaiting guests, she tripped, the tart fell and dessert was delayed. But only long enough for the fallen tart to be recreated and served with aplomb as Tarte des Demoiselles Tatin.

1 cup granulated white
   sugar
1/4 cup water
4 pounds crisp apples,
   peeled and sliced 1/8
   thick
Juice of 1 lemon
4 tablespoons butter, cut
   into bits
Basic Pie Crust dough for
   one 9-inch pie shell,
   page 15
Whipped cream

Preheat the oven to 375°F. Combine 1/3 cup of the sugar and the water in a heavy saucepan and stir constantly over low heat to dissolve the sugar. Raise the heat and cook until the sugar turns a rich caramel color, brushing down any crystals that cling to the sides of the pan with a natural bristle brush. Coat the bottom and sides of a 9- or 10-inch pie plate, preferably glass, 2 to 2-1/2 inches deep with the caramelized sugar and let it harden.

Toss the sliced apples with 1/3 cup of the sugar and the lemon juice. Arrange the most perfect slices on top of the hardened caramel, starting from the center of the plate and working outward. Overlap the slices so the rounded sides are hidden. When the bottom and part of the sides are covered, sprinkle with 1 tablespoon of the sugar and dot with 1 tablespoon of the butter. Arrange half of the remaining apple slices on top and sprinkle with 2 tablespoons of the sugar and dot with 1 tablespoon of the butter. Arrange the remaining apple slices on top, sprinkle with 1 tablespoon of the sugar and dot with the remaining butter.

Roll out the pastry dough into a circle slightly larger than the pie plate and place on top of the apples. Trim the pastry even with the sides of the plate and make a few air holes in the top. Sprinkle the top with the remaining sugar and place on a baking sheet in the preheated oven. Bake for 45 to 60 minutes, or until the pastry is nicely browned.

Remove the tart from the oven and allow to cool for 5 minutes. Place a serving plate on top of the pie plate and invert the tart onto the plate, revealing a lovely mass of caramelized apples. Serve warm or cold, accompanied with whipped cream.
Makes 8 to 10 servings

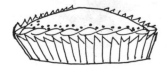

DUTCH PEAR OR APPLE PIE

2 cups peeled and sliced
   pears or apples
1/4 cup frozen orange juice
   concentrate, thawed, if
   using pears
2 tablespoons fresh lemon
   juice, if using apples

3/4 cup granulated white
   sugar
1 cup (1/2 pint) sour cream
1 teaspoon vanilla extract
2 tablespoons flour
1 egg
1/8 teaspoon salt
One 9-inch partially baked
   pie shell, page 15
Lightly whipped cream for
   serving

Streusel
4 tablespoons butter
1/4 cup firmly packed
   brown sugar
1/4 cup granulated white
   sugar
3/4 cup all-purpose white
   flour
Grated zest of 1 orange
1 teaspoon ground cinnamon
1/2 cup lightly toasted
   chopped walnuts

88

Preheat the oven to 350°F. If using pears, put the slices into the orange juice concentrate. If using apples, put the slices into the lemon juice. Combine the sugar, sour cream, vanilla extract, flour, egg and salt and mix well. Stir the mixture into the fruit slices, then transfer to the partially baked pie shell. Bake in the preheated oven until just set, about 25 minutes.

While the pie is baking, prepare the streusel topping. Cream the butter and add the sugars, flour, orange zest, cinnamon and walnuts, blending in thoroughly. Remove the pie from the oven, spread the streusel over the top and return it to the oven to bake until the topping is nicely browned, about 10 to 15 minutes. Serve warm or cold with lightly whipped cream.
Makes 8 to 10 servings

GERMAN NUT TORTE

Basic Pie Crust dough, page 15 (see Note)
1 recipe Almond Cake batter, page 51
3/4 cup granulated white sugar
2 tablespoons light corn syrup
6 tablespoons butter
1/3 cup heavy cream
1-1/2 cups very coarsely chopped lightly toasted walnuts

Preheat the oven to 375°F. Roll out the pie crust dough no more than 1/8 inch thick and line a 10-inch springform pan with it. Fill two thirds full with the cake batter and bake in the preheated oven for 30 to 40 minutes, or until a wooden pick inserted in the center comes forth clean. Remove from the oven and let cool.

While the almond base is baking, combine the sugar and corn syrup in a heavy-bottomed pan and place over medium heat until caramelized. Remove from the heat and stir in the butter. Return the pan to low heat until the butter is completely melted. Add the cream, bring to a boil and fold in the walnuts, blending together well. Remove from the heat and cool to lukewarm.

With a lightly oiled palette knife, spread the topping over the cooled almond base. Refrigerate for at least 30 minutes before serving.
Makes 10 to 12 servings

NOTE Follow the directions for preparing the pie crust dough, but use the following measures: 1/4 pound plus 4 tablespoons butter or 7 tablespoons butter and 5 tablespoons margarine, 1-1/2 cups flour, 1 teaspoon salt and 3 tablespoons water.

FUDGE PIE

Rich, very rich. A must for chocolate lovers.

5 ounces semisweet
    chocolate
10 tablespoons (5 ounces)
    butter
4 eggs
2 cups sugar
1 teaspoon vanilla extract
One 9-inch partially baked
    pie shell, page 15
Whipped cream for serving

Preheat the oven to 375°F. Combine the chocolate and butter in the top pan of a double boiler placed over simmering water and heat until melted. Remove from the heat and cool to room temperature. Mix together the eggs, sugar and vanilla extract and stir in the cooled chocolate-butter mixture. Pour into the partially baked pie shell and bake in the preheated oven for 45 to 60 minutes, or until a wooden pick inserted in the center comes forth clean. Serve with cream.
Makes 8 to 10 servings

NOTE It is important that this pie not be refrigerated, or the top will not remain crusty as it should.

WALNUT PIE

This recipe is from Ms. Becky Blake, a long-time volunteer at the Oakland Museum.

3 eggs, lightly beaten
1/2 cup firmly packed
    brown sugar
1 cup light corn syrup
1/4 teaspoon salt
1/2 teaspoon vanilla extract
1 cup very coarsely chopped
    lightly toasted walnuts
One 9-inch partially baked
    pie shell, page 15
1/2 cup heavy cream,
    whipped
8 to 10 lightly toasted
    perfect walnut halves

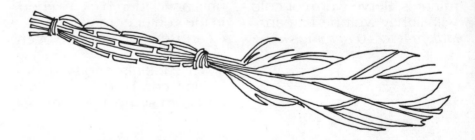

Preheat the oven to 425°F. Mix together thoroughly the eggs, sugar, corn syrup, salt and vanilla extract. Stir in the chopped walnuts and pour into the partially baked pie shell. Bake in the preheated 425°F oven for 10 minutes, then lower heat to 350°F and bake for 35 minutes or until set. Remove from the oven, cool to room temperature and chill.

To serve, cover the top of the pie with a thin layer of whipped cream, or perhaps pipe rosettes of cream around the edge. Garnish with the walnut halves.
Makes 8 to 10 servings

PECAN PIE Substitute 1 cup very coarsely chopped lightly toasted perfect pecan halves for the walnut halves.

AVOCADO PIE

It's hard to imagine just how good avocados—lightly sweetened with honey and flavored with lemon juice—are for dessert unless you have tried them. Such a luxurient texture couldn't be relegated to guacamole forever. Peter Reimuller introduced avocado pie to the Mendocino coast many years ago, and it has been standard potluck fare ever since. I have experimented with Peter's recipe, which originally called for sweetened condensed milk, and here is the result.

1/2 pound kefir cheese
1/2 cup plain yoghurt
2 medium ripe avocados, peeled and mashed
1/4 cup honey
Grated zest of 1 lemon
3 tablespoons fresh lemon juice
One 9-inch prebaked Oatmeal-Honey pie shell, page 16

With an electric mixer, beat together the kefir cheese, yoghurt and avocados. Add the honey and lemon zest and juice and blend well at high speed. Pour into the prebaked crust and chill well before serving.
Makes 8 servings

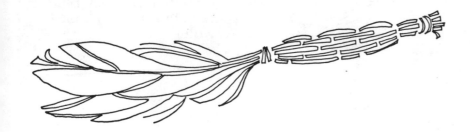

SWEET POTATO PIE

A wonderful treat. I first ate sweet potato pie at a jazz festival in Berkeley, California, in 1969, and it took me nine years to develop a recipe that I liked as much as that first one.

8 ounces cream cheese
1/2 cup honey
4 eggs, beaten
3 cups peeled and mashed
   cooked sweet potatoes
1/2 cup milk, heavy cream,
   plain yoghurt or plain kefir
1-1/4 teaspoons ground
   cinnamon
1/4 teaspoon ground ginger
1/4 teaspoon ground
   nutmeg
1/8 teaspoon ground cloves
2 tablespoons brandy
One 9-inch partially baked
   pie shell, page 15 (see
   Note)

Preheat the oven to 350°F. Cream the cheese, then mix in the honey and eggs. Add the sweet potatoes, liquid of choice, spices and brandy and mix until smooth. Pour into the partially baked pie shell and bake in the pre-heated oven for 45 to 50 minutes, or until a wooden pick inserted in the center comes forth clean.
Makes 8 to 10 servings

NOTE A pie shell made with whole-wheat pastry flour is particularly complementary to this pie.

CHESS PIE

I first became aware of this rich southern pie when asked to make a box lunch dessert for 400...what an introduction!

2 eggs
2/3 cup firmly packed
   brown sugar, or
   1/3 cup honey or malt
   syrup
1/2 teaspoon salt
1 teaspoon ground
   cinnamon
1-1/2 tablespoons
   unbleached or all-purpose
   white flour
1 teaspoon vanilla extract
1 cup heavy cream
1/2 cup sultanas
1 cup pitted dates, chopped
1 cup broken lightly toasted
   pecans
One partially baked 9-inch
   pie shell, page 15
Whipped cream

Preheat the oven to 350°F. Beat the eggs until pale and thick. Beat in the sweetener of choice, salt, cinnamon and flour, then stir in the vanilla extract, cream, raisins, dates and pecans. Spoon the mixture into the partially baked pie shell and bake in the preheated oven for 40 to 50 minutes, or until a knife inserted in the center comes forth clean. Serve warm or chilled with whipped cream.
Makes 8 servings

ROBERT BOYLE'S CHEESECAKE

This is a wonderful cheese-cake. Although everyone says that same thing about which-ever cheesecake recipe they have decided to call their own, this one actually is won-derful if you like the moist, creamy kind versus the drier, cheesier variety. Robert Boyle, former chef at Narsai's, created this favorite cheese-cake. It is lovely served with puréed fruit, such as straw-berries, apricots, raspberries.

Graham-Cracker Crust
  mixture, page 16
1-1/2 pounds cream cheese,
  at room temperature
3/4 cup granulated white
  sugar
2 eggs
1/2 tablespoon vanilla
  extract
Grated zest of 1 lemon

Topping
1 cup (1/2 pint) sour cream
1 egg
1/2 teaspoon vanilla extract
1/4 cup granulated white
  sugar

Preheat the oven to 350°F. Press the cracker crust mixture onto the bottom and sides of a 9-inch spring-form pan. Mix together the cream cheese and sugar until well blended, then thoroughly mix in the eggs. Stir in the vanilla and lemon zest and pour into the prepared pie crust. Place the spring-form pan on a baking sheet in the preheated oven and bake for 25 minutes, or until the cheesecake is just set.

While the cheesecake is baking, prepare the topping by mixing together all of the ingredients until well blended. Remove the cake from the oven and raise the oven temperature to 425°F. Pour the topping onto the cheesecake, return it to the 425°F oven and bake for 15 minutes. Remove from the oven, let cool to room temperature and refrigerate at least 12 hours before serving.
Makes 12 servings

COTTAGE-CHEESE CAKE

This is a healthier version, though no less rich, of Robert's cake. I just didn't have enough cream cheese one day, so with a few substitutions, I arrived at this delicious result.

Oatmeal-Honey Crust mixture or Graham-Cracker Crust mixture, page 16
2 cups (1 pint) cottage cheese
1/2 pound kefir cheese or cream cheese, at room temperature
2 eggs
1/4 cup honey
1 teaspoon vanilla extract
Grated zest of 1/2 lemon

Topping
1 egg
1 cup plain yoghurt
2 tablespoons honey
1/2 teaspoon vanilla extract
3/4 cup stemmed huckleberries, halved and pitted dark cherries or peeled and thinly sliced peaches (optional)

Preheat the oven to 350°F. Press the oatmeal or cracker crust mixture onto the bottom and sides of a 9-inch spring-form pan. Press the cottage cheese through a wire sieve into the bowl of an electric mixer. Add the kefir or cream cheese and mix until smooth. Whip in the eggs and honey, then the vanilla extract and lemon zest. Pour into the prepared pie crust and place on a baking sheet in the preheated oven. Bake for 25 minutes, or until just set.

While the cake is baking, prepare the topping. With a wire whisk, beat together the egg, yoghurt, honey and vanilla extract. Mix in the fruit, if desired. Remove the cake from the oven and raise the oven temperature to 425°F. Pour the topping onto the cheesecake, return it to the 425°F oven and bake for 12 minutes. Remove from the oven, let cool to room temperature and refrigerate at least 12 hours before serving.
Makes 10 servings

SUPER-RICH, VERY CHOCOLATE CHEESECAKE

A wonderful recipe by way of Barry Tasner, food-aficionado extraordinaire. Some advice from Barry: This cake should either be served as a highlight to a very light meal or by itself with good coffee *several hours before* retiring.

Crust
2 cups finely crushed
   chocolate wafers
1/4 teaspoon ground
   cinnamon
4 tablespoons butter, melted

Filling
1-1/2 pounds cream cheese,
   at room temperature
1 cup granulated white
   sugar
4 eggs
1 pound semisweet
   chocolate
4 tablespoons butter
1 teaspoon vanilla extract
2 tablespoons unsweetened
   cocoa powder
3 cups (1-1/2 pints) sour
   cream

Preheat the oven to 350°F. To make the crust, combine the crushed wafers, cinnamon and butter until well mixed and press onto the bottom of a 9-inch spring-form pan.

To make the filling, beat together the cream cheese and sugar until fluffy, then beat in the eggs, one at a time. Combine the chocolate and butter in the top pan of a double boiler placed over simmering water until melted. Mix into the cream cheese-sugar mixture along with the vanilla extract, cocoa powder and sour cream. Pour into the prepared pan and bake in the preheated oven for 45 minutes. Turn the oven off and allow the cake to sit in it for 1 hour. Remove from the oven, cool to room temperature and refrigerate for at least 12 hours before serving. *Makes 10 servings*

BAKLAVA

2 cups lightly toasted mixed
  nuts and seeds, such as
  chopped walnuts, sun-
  flower seeds, sesame
  seeds, sliced almonds
1/2 cup honey
1 teaspoon ground
  cinnamon
1/2 pound filo sheets
  (approximately 15 sheets)
1/2 pound unsalted butter,
  melted and cooled

Syrup
1 cup honey
1 teaspoon ground cloves
1 teaspoon freshly grated
  orange zest
2 teaspoons fresh lemon
  juice
1-1/2 tablespoons brandy

Preheat the oven to 325°F. Combine the nuts and seeds, honey and cinnamon and mix well. Cut the filo sheets in half crosswise and keep those sheets you are not working with covered so that they don't dry out. Layer one fourth of the sheets in an 8-by 12-inch baking dish, brushing each lightly with the melted butter. Spread one fourth of the nut-seed mixture over the top. Cover with more sheets, brushing each of them with butter, then top with one third of the remaining nut-seed mixture. Repeat this two more times, until all of the nut-seed mixture is used. Top with the remaining sheets, brushing each with butter. With a sharp knife, cut through all of the filo sheets to form 16 small diamond-shaped pieces. Bake in the preheated oven for 35 to 45 minutes, or until golden brown.

While the baklava is baking, prepare the syrup. Combine all of the ingredients for the syrup in a small saucepan. Bring to a boil, reduce heat and simmer for 8 minutes. Remove the baklava from the oven and immediately spoon the hot syrup over the top. Allow to cool before serving.
Makes 16 servings

On the Light Side

The perfect, light dessert can be found here—everything from a delicate mousse to a silky cream, from a rich custard to lightly poached fruit, from buttery almond cookies to old-fashioned sugar cookies.

BRANDIED PEACH "MOUSSE"

A texture as light as a mousse will ever have.

3/4 cup honey
1 cup water
8 whole cloves
3 bay leaves
4 medium ripe peaches
1 tablespoon Cognac
1/2 cup heavy cream
2 egg whites

Combine the honey, water, cloves and bay leaves in a saucepan and bring the mixture to a boil. Reduce the heat and simmer for 5 minutes.

While the syrup is simmering, put the peaches into a pot of boiling water for 15 seconds. Remove the peaches from the water and peel them, cut them in half and remove and discard the pits. Place the peaches in the simmering honey-water mixture and simmer for about 5 minutes, basting frequently if they are not completely covered by the syrup. (Do not overcook the peaches or they will take on the flavor of canned peaches.) Remove the saucepan from the heat. Lift the peaches out and refrigerate them until chilled, reserving the poaching liquid.

When the peaches are chilled, purée them in a blender with the Cognac. Set aside. Strain the liquid and gently boil it down until it becomes thick and syrupy, being careful not to let it burn. Measure out 1/2 cup of the syrup and set aside.

Whip the cream until it forms stiff peaks and set aside. Whip the egg whites just until they begin to stiffen. Gradually add the 1/2 cup of reserved hot syrup to the whites, whipping at the highest speed until a stiff, glossy meringue is formed, about 5 minutes. Fold in the whipped cream and the puréed peaches and transfer to individual molds or one large, pretty bowl. Chill for several hours before serving.
Makes 4 or 5 servings

CHOCOLATE MOUSSE

12 ounces semisweet
  chocolate
4 tablespoons unsalted
  butter
2 tablespoons triple-strength
  brewed coffee or Grand
  Marnier
2 egg yolks
8 egg whites
1/2 cup granulated white
  sugar
1-1/2 cups heavy cream
1/4 cup confectioners'
  sugar
1 tablespoon vanilla
  extract
1 tablespoon Grand Marnier
  (optional)

Combine the chocolate and butter in the top pan of a double boiler placed over simmering water and heat until melted. Remove from the heat and stir in the coffee or Grand Marnier and the egg yolks; set aside.

In an electric mixer, beat the egg whites until they form soft peaks. Add the granulated sugar, a table-poon at a time, beating well after each addition. Continue beating for 5 more minutes, or until whites are very stiff. With a wire whisk, fold about one fourth of the whites into the chocolate mixture to lighten it, then fold in the remaining whites very carefully. They need not be blended in completely. Place in the refrigerator for about 2 hours until the mixture is very thick, stirring it once about every 30 minutes.

Whip the cream with the confectioners' sugar, vanilla extract and Grand Marnier, if used, until stiff peaks form. Fold two thirds of the cream into the chocolate. With a pastry bag fitted with a large plain tip, pipe the mousse into individual dessert dishes, champagne glasses or a pretty bowl. With a pastry bag fitted with a large star tip, decorate the mousse with the remaining whipped cream. Refrigerate until ready to serve.
Makes 8 to 10 servings

BRANDY-BANANA CREAM

This cream can be used in a number of ways. Spoon it into individual champagne glasses; pipe a rosette of whipped cream on top and garnish with toasted sliced almonds. Or make a garnish of needlethreads (page 49) from the lemon or lime before juicing, which would make a more classic garnish. This cream is also lovely spooned over pound cake at tea time, or if it seems to be able to hold its shape (perhaps by adding extra cream cheese or a bit of gelatin sponged with the fresh citrus juice), you can use it as a filling for Virtuous Vanilla, forming Beatific Banana.

3/4 pound cream cheese, at
    room temperature
1/2 cup kefir cheese or sour
    cream
1/4 cup honey
2 tablespoons brandy
2 large ripe bananas,
    mashed
2 tablespoons fresh lemon
    or lime juice

In an electric mixer, whip the
cream cheese until smooth
and fluffy. Add the kefir
cheese or sour cream, honey
and brandy and beat again
until smooth. Then add the
mashed bananas and citrus
juice and beat until thoroughly
blended. Refrigerate until firm.
Makes 6 servings

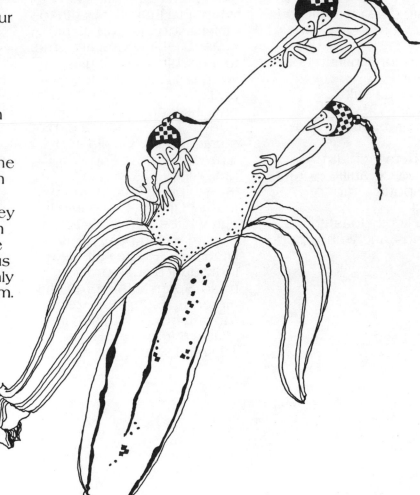

COFFEE TORTONI

A favorite dessert at the Oakland Museum Restaurant.

2 tablespoons instant coffee
  powder
1/4 teaspoon salt
2 egg whites
3/4 cup granulated white
  sugar
2 cups heavy cream
2 teaspoons vanilla extract
1/4 teaspoon almond
  extract
3/4 cup lightly toasted
  almonds, finely chopped

Add the coffee powder and
salt to the egg whites and
whip until they just begin to
stiffen. Add 1/4 cup of the
sugar, a tablespoon at a time,
to the whites, continuing to
whip until they are quite stiff
and glossy. Whip the cream
until thick and frothy. Then
add the remaining 1/2 cup of
sugar and the vanilla and
almond extracts and whip
until stiff peaks form. Fold
the whipped cream and two
thirds of the almonds into the
egg whites. Fancifully spoon
or pipe with a pastry bag
fitted with a large star tip into
individual dishes or a large
mold. Sprinkle the remaining
almonds on top. Freeze, removing just before serving.
*Makes 6 large or
12 small servings*

COLD SABAYON
(Sabayon Glacé or
Zabaglione Freddo)

This French and Italian favorite is wonderful by itself, as
a sauce for pound cake, or
with fresh strawberries or a
poached pear or peach half.
You can substitute Grand
Marnier, Amaretto or any liqueur of your choice for the
Marsala.

6 egg yolks
1/2 cup granulated white
  sugar
1/3 to 1/2 cup Marsala
1/2 cup heavy cream

In a *bain marie,* whisk the yolks, sugar and Marsala over medium heat until quite thick and light. Remove from the heat and mix an additional 5 minutes with an electric mixer. Refrigerate for 2 hours. Whip the cream until stiff peaks form and fold into the chilled mixture. Serve in individual dishes or a large, pretty bowl.
Makes 4 or 5 servings

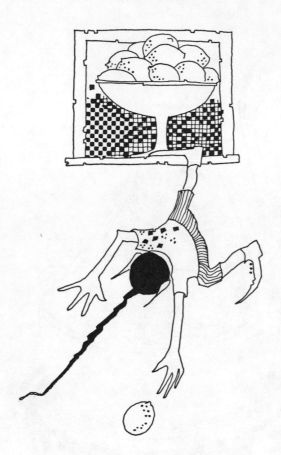

LEMON "MOUSSE"

A light, refreshing dessert after a heavy meal.

1 cup heavy ceam
2 tablespoons confectioners' sugar
1 teaspoon vanilla extract
1 recipe Lemon Filling, page 39, cooled to room temperature
Needlethreads of orange and lemon, page 49

Combine the cream, sugar and vanilla extract and whip until stiff peaks form. Fold half of the whipped cream into the cooled lemon filling. Spoon into individual dishes or champagne glasses. With a pastry bag fitted with a large star tip, pipe rosettes of the reserved whipped cream on top. Garnish with needlethreads.
Makes 4 to 6 servings

LEMON-ORANGE MOUSSE

A very versatile mousse recipe. Once chef Morris Kau of Narsai's suggested using puréed apricots in place of the orange juice. Just as lovely.

2 egg yolks
2 whole eggs
5 tablespoons granulated white sugar
1/4 cup fresh lemon juice
1/4 cup fresh orange juice
1 tablespoon unflavored gelatin
3 tablespoons water
2 egg whites
1-1/2 cups heavy cream
Needlethreads of lemon and orange, page 49

Combine the egg yolks, whole eggs, sugar and citrus juices in the top pan of a double boiler placed over simmering water and beat constantly until thickened. Remove from the heat. Dissolve the gelatin in the water and mix into the hot egg mixture until well blended. Cool just until the mixture begins to jell. (To test, push a spoon through the center of the mixture to see if it divides along either side of its bowl.) Beat the egg whites until stiff peaks form; then beat the cream until stiff peaks form. Fold the egg whites and two thirds of the whipped cream into the jelled mixture and chill 5 minutes. Spoon into individual dishes or a mold. Serve garnished with the remaining whipped cream and needlethreads of lemon and orange.
Makes 6 servings

VARIATION Flavor the whipped cream for garnishing with vanilla extract or Grand Marnier to taste.

STRAWBERRY CREAM

This is a "mousse" for people who cannot eat eggs. I created it when I needed an alternative to whipped cream and sliced strawberries for a cake. You can substitute other fresh fruit for the strawberries, such as kiwis, raspberries, blackberries, peaches, or dark, sweet cherries. Excellent served alone or spread between the layers of a vanilla *génoise* for a variation on strawberry shortcake.

2 cups puréed strawberries
1/4 cup honey
1 cup heavy cream
1 teaspoon vanilla extract
Mint sprigs

Combine the strawberries and honey in a saucepan and bring to a boil. Reduce the heat and simmer, stirring occasionally, for 25 minutes. Remove from the heat, cool to room temperature and refrigerate until chilled thoroughly.

Whip the cream with the vanilla extract until stiff peaks form. Fold the cream into the chilled strawberry mixture and refrigerate again until thoroughly chilled. Serve garnished with fresh mint sprigs.
Makes 6 to 8 servings

CUSTARD

A perfect dessert by itself, with fruit (*crème renversée*) or with caramel sauce (*crème caramel*). To ensure a creamy texture, bake at a low oven temperature, and always bake in a pan with water to a depth of two thirds the depth of the custard dish. For a *very* rich custard, substitute the egg yolks for the whole eggs.

4 whole eggs, or
   1/2 cup egg yolks (approximately 6)
1/3 cup granulated white sugar, or
   1/4 cup honey
1/3 teaspoon vanilla extract
1-1/3 cups half-and-half cream
2/3 cup milk

Preheat the oven to 300°F. Whisk the eggs or egg yolks with the sugar or honey, then whisk in the half-and-half cream and the milk. Pour through a fine wire strainer into individual custard cups or a large baking dish. Place the cups or dish in a pan filled with water to a depth of two thirds the depth of the cups or dish. Bake in the preheated oven about 1-1/2 hours or until a knife inserted in the center comes forth clean. Immediately remove from the oven and place the cups or dish on a wire rack to cool. Serve warm or cold. *Makes 4 to 6 servings*

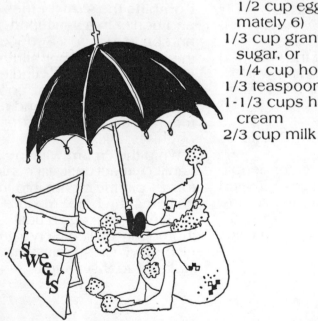

CREME CARAMEL

This is really *crème renversée au caramel*—or upside-down custard with caramel sauce.

1 recipe uncooked Custard, preceding
1/2 cup granulated white sugar
1 tablespoon water

Preheat the oven to 300°F. Prepare the custard just to the point where it is to be strained through the wire sieve. In a heavy-bottomed pan, combine the sugar and water over low heat and heat until the sugar is dissolved. With a natural bristle brush dipped in cold water, wipe down any sugar crystals clinging to the sides of the pan. Raise the heat and continue to cook until the mixture turns a light brown. Periodically, wipe down the sides of the pan with the brush dipped in cold water to prevent the sugar from crystallizing instead of caramelizing. As soon as the caramel is the color you wish (the darker the color, the more intense the caramel flavor), distribute it evenly among the custard cups. Then distribute the custard among the cups, straining it through the wire sieve. Bake as directed for Custard and cool on a wire rack. To unmold, run a knife blade carefully around the edge of each cup and turn out into a champagne glass or onto an attractive dish.
Makes 4 to 6 servings

CREME RENVERSEE

Follow the recipe for Custard, preceding. Serve unmolded, inverted on a serving dish. *Crème renversée* is often accompanied with fresh fruit, some of it puréed and some of it whole, flavored with a liqueur and a bit of sugar. This is called *crème renversée aux fruits.* It is also good served with Apricot Sauce, Strawberry Sauce, Spiced Orange Segments, jams thinned with liqueur and Apricot Glaze.

APPLESAUCE

My favorite applesauce. It is quite rich and is used, in a varied form, in Tarte aux Poires.

4 pounds crisp cooking apples, peeled, cored and coarsely chopped
1/4 cup apricot preserves
1 tablespoon vanilla extract
2/3 cup granulated sugar
3 tablespoons butter

Place the apples in a heavy-bottomed saucepan. Cover the pan with a tightly fitting lid and cook over *very low* heat about 20 minutes, or until the apples are tender. (No water is necessary, as the apples will not scorch if the heat is low and the pot tightly covered.) Stir in the apricot preserves, vanilla extract, sugar and butter until well blended. Serve warm.
Makes 4 cups; 6 to 8 servings

APPLE CRISP

Always a favorite dessert when I was growing up. My mother had a hard time keeping her children from sampling the topping when the crisp was just out of the oven. This is a variation on my mother's basic recipe.

8 to 10 cooking apples, peeled, cored and sliced
Juice of 1 lemon

Topping
1/2 pound butter
2/3 cup honey
4 cups rolled oats
1/2 cup chopped lightly toasted walnuts or almonds
1/2 cup lightly toasted sunflower seeds
1-1/2 cups unbleached or all-purpose white flour
2 teaspoons ground cinnamon
1 teaspoon ground allspice
1 cup fresh orange juice

Preheat the oven to 350°F. Combine the apples and lemon juice, toss lightly and set aside. To make the topping, melt together the honey and butter, then combine with the oats, nuts, sunflower seeds, flour, cinnamon and allspice and mix well. Arrange the apple slices in a 9- by 13-inch pan and cover them with the topping mixture. Pour the orange juice evenly over the top, cover and bake in the preheated oven for 30 minutes. Uncover and bake 15 minutes longer.
Makes 8 to 12 servings

CREMA D'OPORTO

2/3 cup granulated white sugar
1 tablespoon water
2-1/4 cups half-and-half cream, scalded
5 egg yolks
1/4 cup Port wine

Preheat the oven to 300°F. In a heavy-bottomed pan, combine the sugar and water over low heat and heat until the sugar is dissolved. With a natural bristle brush dipped in cold water, wipe down any sugar crystals clinging to the sides of the pan. Raise the heat and continue to cook until the mixture turns a light brown. Periodically, wipe down the sides of the pan with the brush dipped in cold water to prevent the sugar from crystallizing instead of caramelizing. Remove the caramelized sugar from the heat and stir it into the scalded half-and-half cream, mixing it in well. Whisk together the egg yolks and the Port, then whisk in a small amount of the hot milk-sugar mixture. Now whisk the yolk mixture into the milk-sugar mixture and pour it through a wire sieve into 4 or 5 custard cups or individual ramekins. Place the cups or ramekins in a pan filled with water to a depth of two thirds the depth of the cups or ramekins. Bake in the pre-heated oven about 1 hour, or until a knife inserted in the center comes forth clean. Immediately remove from the oven and place the cups on a wire rack to cool. Serve warm preferably, or at room temperature.
Makes 4 or 5 servings

BAKED FRESH FIGS

12 fresh purple figs
1/2 cup frozen apple juice
  concentrate, thawed
Ground cinnamon

Topping
1 cup sour cream, plain
  yoghurt or kefir cheese
2 tablespoons frozen apple
  juice concentrate, thawed
3 tablespoons Grand
  Marnier

Preheat the oven to 350°F.
With the tines of a fork, prick
each fig in a few places.

Place the figs in a buttered
baking dish and pour over
the apple juice concentrate.
Cover the dish and bake in
the preheated oven for 25
minutes, basting with liquid
in the dish. Remove from the
oven and dust the figs lightly
with cinnamon.

To make the topping, mix
together the sour cream, apple juice concentrate and
Grand Marnier until well
blended. Spoon the mixture
over the figs just before serving, either warm or at room
temperature.
Makes 4 to 6 servings

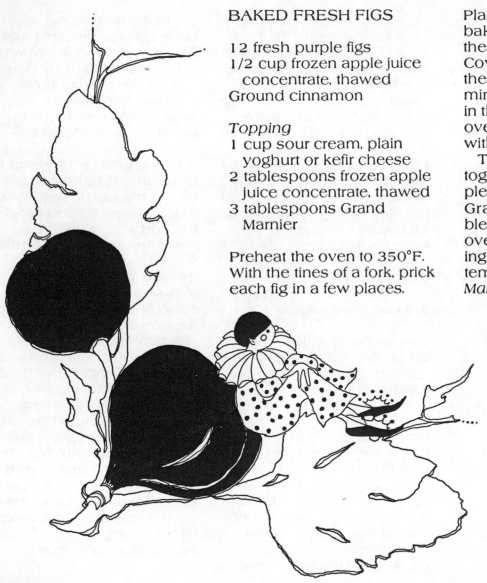

110

SPICED ORANGES

A palate cleanser that leaves you feeling satisfied rather than stuffed. Quite nice after a Moroccan feast of *bastilla* or an Indian curry.

Oranges
Spiced Orange Syrup,
  page 36, boiling
Whipped cream
Needlethreads of lemon and
  orange, page 49

Allow 1 orange for each guest, plus a few extras. Remove the peel and all traces of pith from the oranges, leaving them round and nicely shaped. Place in a shallow bowl and add the boiling orange syrup to cover. Allow the oranges to macerate, refrigerated, at least overnight and preferably for 2 days. Serve with some of the soaking syrup, whipped cream and a garnish of needlethreads. Provide each guest with a fork and knife for easy eating.

APRICOT KISEL

A wonderful Russian fruit pudding. I worked with this recipe until it could be successfully prepared without any sweeteners. The resulting taste is extremely flavorful, almost "haunting," and the consistency is perfect enough to use as a sauce as well.

1 cup dried apricots
One 6-ounce can frozen
  apple juice concentrate,
  thawed
1-1/4 cups water
Grated zest of 1 lemon
Plain yoghurt
Chopped lightly toasted nuts
  (optional)

Put the apricots, apple juice concentrate, water and lemon zest in a saucepan placed over very high heat. When the mixture comes to a boil, remove from the heat, cool to room temperature and refrigerate overnight. The next day, purée the mixture in the blender and spoon into individual bowls or champagne glasses. Garnish each serving with a dollop of yoghurt and a sprinkling of nuts, if desired.
Makes 4 servings

FRUITED YOGHURT

Quite nice by itself or as a sauce over a spice cake or nut bread.

3 cups plain yoghurt
1 ripe banana, mashed
1/4 cup honey
1 teaspoon vanilla extract
Juice of 1/2 lemon or lime
2 cups sliced pitted plums
1/2 cup halved pitted
  cherries

With a wire whisk or an electric mixer, beat together the yoghurt, banana, honey, vanilla extract and lemon or lime juice until well blended. Fold in the plums and cherries and chill at least 2 hours before serving.
Makes 6 servings

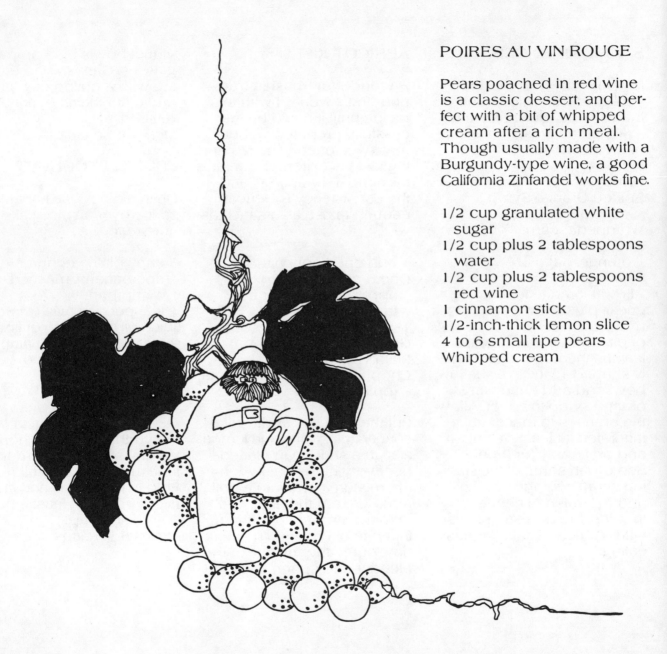

POIRES AU VIN ROUGE

Pears poached in red wine is a classic dessert, and perfect with a bit of whipped cream after a rich meal. Though usually made with a Burgundy-type wine, a good California Zinfandel works fine.

1/2 cup granulated white
   sugar
1/2 cup plus 2 tablespoons
   water
1/2 cup plus 2 tablespoons
   red wine
1 cinnamon stick
1/2-inch-thick lemon slice
4 to 6 small ripe pears
Whipped cream

Combine the sugar, water, wine, cinnamon stick and lemon slice in a medium-sized saucepan placed over moderate heat and heat, stirring, until the sugar is dissolved. Peel the pears, leaving the stems in place but removing the bottom bit of core, and immediately stand them, stem ends up, in the syrup. Cover the saucepan and simmer about 20 minutes, basting once or twice. Transfer the pears to a deep serving dish and simmer the liquid until it is reduced to the consistency of a light syrup. Pour the syrup over the pears, let cool to room temperature and chill. Serve chilled with whipped cream.
Makes 4 to 6 servings

SPICED ITALIAN PRUNE PLUMS IN RED WINE

This late summer fruit has an advantage over other plums in that it is "freestone"—the pit easily lifts from the flesh. The flesh is also firm enough to keep its shape when poached. Halved peaches would make a nice variation.

16 Italian prune plums, halved and pitted
6 ounces frozen apple juice concentrate, thawed
Red wine
2 cinnamon sticks
4 whole cloves
4 whole allspice
Heavy cream or plain yoghurt

Place the plums in a saucepan with the apple juice concentrate and enough red wine to completely cover the fruit. Add the cinnamon sticks, cloves and allspice and simmer, covered with the lid slightly ajar, for 10 to 20 minutes, or until the plums are tender. Serve warm or cold with some of the poaching liquid spooned over the top. Pass a bowl of cream or yoghurt.
Makes 4 servings

HONEY-BAKED PEARS

3 tablespoons fresh lemon
  juice
3/4 teaspoon ground
  cinnamon
1/2 cup honey
1/2 cup lightly toasted
  sunflower seeds
1/4 cup dried currants
4 ripe pears, peeled, cored
  and halved lengthwise
2 tablespoons butter

Preheat the oven to 350°F.
Combine the lemon juice,
cinnamon, honey, sunflower
seeds and currants and mix
well. Place the pears, rounded
side down, in a buttered
baking dish. Place an equal
amount of the honey mixture
in the cavity of each pear
half and dot each with an
equal amount of butter. Bake
in the preheated oven about
35 minutes, or until the fruit is
tender, basting occasionally
with the juices in the dish.
Serve warm.
Makes 4 to 8 servings

ALMOND CHRISTMAS COOKIES

Veronica made these wonderful cookies for giving one Christmas.

1/2 pound butter, at room temperature
1 cup granulated white sugar
1 teaspoon vanilla extract
2 cups *sifted* white pastry flour
1/4 cup ground lightly toasted almonds
24 to 30 lightly toasted whole almonds

Preheat the oven to 350°F. Cream together the butter and sugar until very light and fluffy. Add the vanilla extract, flour and ground almonds, mixing well to form a soft but firm cookie dough. Form the dough into walnut-sized balls and place the balls on buttered baking sheets. Top each ball with a whole almond, pressing it in gently. Bake in the preheated oven for about 10 minutes, or until lightly golden.
Makes 24 to 30 cookies

BUTTER COOKIES

These rich cookies were developed from the recipe for Sweet Pastry dough. You can vary this recipe by using a flavoring other than vanilla, by the addition of chocolate or almond paste, or by topping with raspberry jam or a pecan half. You can even sandwich two together with a filling of butter cream or whipped cream cheese.

1/2 pound butter, at room temperature
2/3 cup granulated white sugar
1/2 teaspoon vanilla extract
1/4 cup fresh lemon juice
Grated zest of 1/2 lemon
1-1/4 cups whole-wheat pastry or unbleached white flour, or as needed
Heavy cream, if needed
Raspberry jam (optional)

Preheat the oven to 350°F. Cream together the butter and sugar until light and fluffy. Add the vanilla extract, lemon juice and lemon zest. Add the flour, mixing until well blended.

You can form the dough for baking in either of two ways: with your hands into walnut-sized balls or piped from a pastry bag through a large star tip to form rosettes. If you are going to form the dough into balls, it should be firm; to form rosettes it should be softer. Bake a sample cookie. If you like the shape it takes in the oven, proceed to bake them all off. If the cookie is too soft, add a bit more flour; if it is too firm, add a bit of heavy cream, a teaspoon at a time. Bake the formed cookies on a buttered or parchment paper-lined baking sheet in the preheated oven for 12 to 15 minutes, or until edges just begin to brown. If you have chosen to pipe the cookies, when you remove them from the oven press the center of the rosette gently and place a dab of jam in the indentation. Allow the cookies to cool for a minute before removing from the baking sheet so that they do not lose their shape.
Makes approximately 24

ALMOND BUTTER COOKIES

7 ounces almond paste
1/2 pound butter, at room temperature
1/4 cup malt syrup or honey
1 teaspoon vanilla extract
1/4 teaspoon almond extract
Grated zest of 1/2 orange
1-1/4 to 1-1/2 cups whole-wheat pastry or unbleached white flour
1 egg white, lightly beaten
1/2 cup lightly toasted sliced almonds

Preheat the oven to 350°F. Cream together the almond paste and butter until smooth and fluffy. Mix in the malt syrup or honey. When well incorporated, mix in the vanilla and almond extracts, orange zest and flour (see Note), blending well.

As with Butter Cookies, page 115, you can either form the dough into balls or pipe it from a pastry bag. If you choose to pipe them, use a 1/2-inch plain tip and form pencil shapes about 2 inches long, leaving 1 inch between the cookies to allow for spreading. The cookies should be arranged on a buttered or parchment paper-lined baking sheet. Make a sample cookie and adjust the dough with more flour or a bit of cream as described in the Butter Cookies recipe. When you have formed all of the cookies, coat them lightly with egg white and sprinkle each with a few sliced almonds. Bake in the preheated oven for 12 to 15 minutes for balls, 10 to 12 minutes for pencil shapes, or until the edges just begin to brown. Allow the cookies to cool for a minute before removing from the baking sheet so that they do not lose their shape. *Makes 24 to 36*

NOTE Use the greater amount of flour indicated if forming into balls, the lesser amount if forming with a pastry bag.

CHOCOLATE BUTTER COOKIES

2 ounces semisweet
   chocolate
2 tablespoons liqueur
   (Káhlua, Grand Marnier,
   Cognac or one of choice)
1/2 pound butter, at room
   temperature
2/3 cup granulated white
   sugar
1/2 teaspoon vanilla extract
1-3/4 cups whole-wheat
   pastry or unbleached
   white flour
Chocolate chips or lightly
   toasted almond slices
   (optional)

Preheat the oven to 350°F. In the top of a double boiler placed over simmering water, melt together the chocolate and liqueur. Remove from the heat and set aside. Cream together the butter and sugar until light and fluffy. Mix in the vanilla extract and flour until almost blended. Then add the melted chocolate and mix well.

As with Butter Cookies, page 115, you can either form the dough into balls or pipe it from a pastry bag through a large star tip to form rosettes. The cookies should be arranged on a buttered and floured or parchment paper-lined baking sheet. Make a sample cookie and adjust the dough with more flour or a bit of cream as described in the Butter Cookies recipe. When you have formed all of the cookies, place a chocolate chip or an almond slice in the center of each, if desired. Bake in the preheated oven for 12 to 15 minutes, or until *lightly* crusted on top. Allow the cookies to cool for a minute before removing them from the baking sheet so that they do not lose their shape.
Makes approximately 24

VARIATION Pipe the cookies into small rosettes and reduce cooking time to 8 to 10 minutes. When the cookies have cooled completely, sandwich them together with a bit of Chocolate or Mocha Butter Cream (page 31).

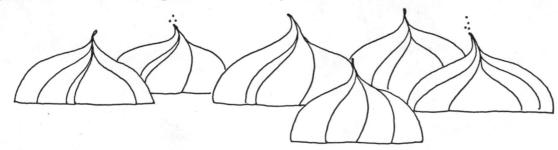

ENGLISH TOFFEE COOKIES

Another excellent recipe from the Oakland Museum Restaurant volunteers.

1/2 pound butter, at room temperature
2/3 cup firmly packed brown sugar
1/3 cup granulated white sugar
1 egg, separated
2 cups all-purpose or unbleached white or whole-wheat pastry flour
1 teaspoon ground cinnamon
1/3 cup lightly toasted sliced almonds

Preheat the oven to 350°F. Line an 11- by 16-inch baking pan with parchment paper or butter and flour it.

Cream together the butter and sugars until smooth and fluffy. Add the egg yolk, and mix in thoroughly. Stir in the flour and cinnamon until well blended.

Put a small amount of granulated white sugar on the palms of your hands and press the dough into the prepared pan in an even layer. (Replace the sugar on your hands as needed to prevent the dough from sticking to them.) Lightly beat the egg white and spread on top of the dough to completely cover the surface. Sprinkle the almonds evenly over the top. Bake in the preheated oven for 25 minutes, or until golden. Remove from the oven and cut into 1-inch-long diamond shapes while still hot.
Makes approximately 48

NOTE These cookies freeze very successfully.

MOLASSES SUGAR COOKIES

These cookies were the mainstay of my diet during my college years. They look exactly as a cookie "should" look in my mind—perfectly round, with a beautiful cracked pattern on top revealing the chewy center beneath the crisp surface. One woman I know makes these cookies with butter, which produces a better flavor but the cookies lose their cracks, and thus their personality. The choice is yours.

1/4 pound margarine
1/4 cup vegetable shortening
1 cup granulated white
   sugar
1/4 cup molasses
1 egg
2 teaspoons baking soda
1 teaspoon ground
   cinnamon
1/2 teaspoon ground cloves
1/2 teaspoon ground ginger
1/2 teaspoon salt
2 cups unbleached or
   all-purpose white flour
Granulated white sugar

Cream together the margarine, shortening and sugar until light and fluffy. Add the molasses and the egg, beating well to mix thoroughly. Add the baking soda, cinnamon, cloves, ginger and salt, mix well, and then mix in the flour and form into a ball. Chill the dough for at least 20 minutes. If you cut back on this time, the dough will be much too sticky to handle easily. While the dough is chilling, preheat the oven to oven to 350°F.

Remove the dough from the refrigerator and form it into walnut-sized balls. Roll each ball in the granulated sugar to coat all surfaces lightly and place on buttered baking sheets 2 inches apart. Bake in the preheated oven for 8 to 10 minutes, or until golden.
Makes 36

NOTE To make these cookies with butter, omit the margarine and vegetable shortening and cream 1/4 pound plus 4 tablespoons butter with the sugar.

GINGER COOKIES

This is just a variation on the preceding recipe for Molasses Sugar Cookies. You may make these large or small, leave them plain or sandwich them together with a filling of whipped cream cheese. When ground into crumbs, they make a delicious ginger-cookie crumb crust.

You can substitute a half cup of honey for the cup of granulated white sugar. The result will be a moister, more cakelike cookie, without the cracks. (To use this variation for a crumb crust, you will need to let the cookies dry out a bit before grinding them.)

Follow the recipe for Molasses Sugar Cookies, page 119, making the following changes in the spice measures: 2 to 3 teaspoons ground ginger, 1/2 teaspoon ground cinnamon, and 1/4 teaspoon ground cloves.

HAMANTASHEN

I grew up eating hamantashen at my grandmother's house and at Purim festivals at the Jewish Community Center. It was not until I was 20, however, that I first attempted to make them myself, and then not again for another decade. They really deserve to be made more often, especially with this easy recipe.

2 cups unbleached or
   all-purpose white flour
1-1/2 teaspoons baking
   powder
1/4 cup granulated white
   sugar
Pinch of salt
Grated zest of 1/2 lemon
2 eggs
2 tablespoons vegetable oil
1 to 1-1/2 cups filling of
   choice*

Sift together the flour and baking powder. Stir in the sugar, salt and lemon zest, then stir in the eggs and oil.

On a lightly floured board, knead a few minutes until smooth. Form into a ball and chill for 10 minutes. Preheat the oven to 375°F.

Lightly dust your work surface with granulated sugar and roll out the dough 1/8 inch thick. Cut the dough into circles 3-1/2 inches in diameter and place about 2 tablespoons of filling in the center of each circle. Draw up 2 sides of each circle and then pull the third side up and across to meet them, pinching the edges together to form a triangle. Place the filled cookies on a lightly buttered baking sheet and chill another 10 minutes. Bake in the preheated oven for 15 to 20 minutes, or until golden.
Makes approximately 12

*Poppy-Seed Filling (page 40), Almond-Cheese Filling (page 39) or Old World Cheese Filling (page 40) would all be appropriate, or use Apricot Preserves, page 47.

MERINGUE MUSHROOMS

These are wonderful for decorating a *bûche de noël* or for arranging along with *petits fours*. To form them properly, you must have mastered the use of a pastry bag.

1/2 recipe Basic Meringue, page 25
1/2 cup Chocolate Butter Cream, page 31
1/4 cup unsweetened cocoa powder

Preheat the oven to 200°F. Prepare the meringue mixture and fill a pastry bag fitted with a 1/4-inch plain tip. Line a baking sheet with parchment paper or lightly butter and flour it. Pipe an equal number of 2 different forms onto the sheet: First, form pointed rounds, like candy kisses, to be used for stems. Second, make small rounded forms, 1 to 1-1/2 inches in diameter, to be used for caps. Any "tails" (points) on the caps may be flattened with your finger that has been first dipped in cold water.

Bake in the preheated oven for 1 to 1-1/2 hours, or until completely dry. Remove from the oven, and with the point of a small knife blade, make a small opening in the center of the bottom of each cap. Fill a pastry bag fitted with a small fluted tip with the butter cream. Decoratively fill the opening in each cap with some butter cream and press a stem into it to form the mushroom. Stand the mushrooms up next to one another and sift a light dusting of the cocoa powder over the tops.

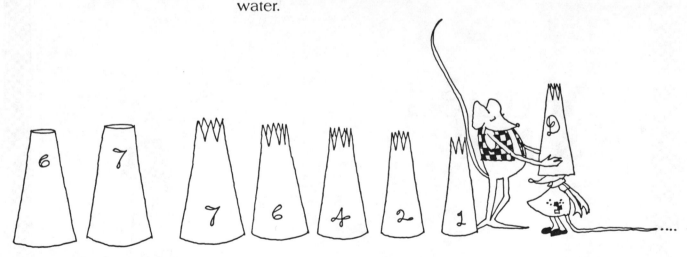

Yeasted
& Not

The moment someone mentions "yeast," many a dessert maker steps back. If you are unfamiliar with the mysteries of yeast, this chapter is a good place to start. The basic coffee-cake dough, which can be transformed into a number of delicious sweets, is easy to make. It is important, however, that your yeast be fresh (check the date on the package) and that it be handled properly. Yeast loves sugar and sweet, and cozy temperatures. It does not like salt, oil, drafts or extremes of hot and cold.

You must also properly knead the dough. That's what gives yeast breads and pastries the non-crumbly texture that distinguishes them from cakes: They hold together, and when you pull them apart, there is always the question of which side will end up larger. As to how long to knead dough? There are almost as many opinions as cooks, so you will just have to learn to judge through practice.

The other cakes and tea breads in this chapter do not call for yeast. A bit of baking soda or baking powder creates their "lift." These recipes represent the easy side of dessert making, rarely requiring frosting, special garnishes or whole afternoons. And yet, they do satisfy the need for something sweet. They also promise to perfume the air.

Go ahead, invite someone special in for tea. . . .

BASIC
COFFEE-CAKE DOUGH

This coffee-cake dough is designed to be made with unbleached or all-purpose white flour or half white and half whole-wheat flour. The "sponge" method is used for making this dough because it results in a lighter cake.

5 tablespoons granulated
   white sugar
1/4 teaspoon ground ginger
2-1/4 cups lukewarm milk
   (110° to 115°F)

1 tablespoon active dry
  yeast
5 cups flour, or as needed
  (see introductory note)
4 egg yolks, or 2 whole
  eggs, lightly beaten
3 tablespoons butter,
  melted
1 tablespoon salt
1/4 pound butter, softened
  and cut in bits

In a small bowl, combine 1 tablespoon of the sugar, the ginger, 1/4 cup of the milk and the yeast, stir to dissolve and let stand until bubbly.

(Note: This is the stage where you can tell if your yeast is alive and therefore usable. If it fails to rise in the presence of the sugar and you are sure the milk was not too warm to kill it, begin again with fresh yeast. If the milk *was* too warm, begin again with fresh yeast and watch the temperature more carefully.)

In a large mixing bowl, combine the remaining 2 cups of milk, the remaining 4 tablespoons of sugar and 2 cups of the flour. Beat in the yeast mixture until thoroughly combined. Cover with a tea towel and let rise in a warm place until double in bulk. This is the "sponge."

With a wooden spoon, stir in the egg yolks or whole eggs, melted butter, salt and the remaining flour. When well combined, turn out onto a floured board and knead the dough until it is springy to the touch and no longer sticky, about 5 to 10 minutes. (If you have an electric mixer with a dough hook, the ingredients can be combined and kneaded in the mixer.) Now knead the butter bits into the dough to enrich it, adding more flour as needed to prevent the dough from becoming sticky.

Form the dough into a ball and place in a well-oiled bowl. Turn the dough to coat all surfaces and cover with a lightly dampened tea towel. Let rise in a warm place until double in bulk.

Turn out onto a well-floured surface, punch down and then shape, fill, let rise and bake as directed in recipes.
Makes dough for
3 coffee cakes

BIENSTITCH

When I worked at St. Orres Inn making their breakfast pastries, these were the ones guests always asked if they could purchase to take home to their friends.

1 recipe Basic Coffee-Cake Dough, preceding
1 recipe Old World Cheese Filling, page 40, or Apricot-Banana Filling, page 38-39

Topping
1/4 pound butter
1/2 cup honey
1/2 cup granulated white sugar
3/4 cup lightly toasted sliced almonds or walnut halves

Prepare the coffee-cake dough. While the dough is rising, prepare the filling and the topping. To make the topping, combine the butter, honey and sugar in a saucepan and cook over low heat, stirring occasionally, until the sugar dissolves and the butter is melted. Raise the heat and cook rapidly for 1 minute. Add the nuts and cook 1 minute longer. Remove from the heat and set aside.

After the dough has risen, divide it into thirds. Working with 1 portion at a time and keeping the other ones covered with a tea towel, roll it out on a floured board into a circle 12 inches in diameter and 1/4 inch thick. Spread the circle with one third of the filling and lift it into a parchment paper-lined 9-inch pie or cake pan, bringing the edges into the center. Top with one third of the topping and repeat with the remaining dough portions. Let rise in a warm place until double in size.

Preheat the oven to 350°F. When the pastries have risen, bake in the preheated oven for 35 minutes, or until nicely browned.

These cakes freeze well. To serve for breakfast, remove from the freezer the night before and thaw in the refrigerator. Reheat, wrapped in foil, in a 300°F oven for about 25 minutes.
Makes 3 coffee cakes

STICKY CINNAMON BUNS

1 recipe Basic Coffee-Cake
   Dough, page 124-125
Melted butter
Ground cinnamon
Ground cardamom (optional)
Raisins (optional)
Brown sugar
Grated orange zest
Coarsely chopped lightly
   toasted walnuts

Topping
1/4 pound plus 4 table-
   spoons butter, melted
1 cup honey
3/4 to 1 cup firmly packed
   brown sugar
1-1/2 cups chopped lightly
   toasted walnuts

Prepare the coffee-cake dough. After it has risen, roll it out on a floured surface into a large rectangle about 1/4 inch thick. Liberally brush the rectangle with melted butter and generously sprinkle with cinnamon, cardamom, raisins, sugar, orange zest and walnuts. Starting at a long side, roll up jelly-roll fashion and cut into 36 slices.

Combine all of the ingredients for the topping and equally distribute it among 36 buttered muffin-well tins. Place the slices, cut side down, in the muffin wells. Let rise in a warm place until double in size.

While the dough is rising, preheat the oven to 350°F. Bake in the preheated oven for 20 to 25 minutes, or until nicely browned. Remove from the oven, and while still warm, run a knife around the edge of each muffin, then turn upside down onto a baking sheet. Do not remove the muffin tins for at least 5 minutes to allow all the sticky mixture to adhere to the rolls. *Makes 36 rolls*

NOTE For larger rolls, cut into 1-1/2-inch slices and place in cake pans that have been coated evenly with the topping mixture.

FILLED BRAID

1 recipe Basic Coffee-Cake Dough, page 124-125
1 recipe Almond-Cheese Filling, page 39, Apricot-Banana Filling, page 38-39, Old World Cheese Filling, page 40, or Spiced Raisin Filling, page 41
1 egg, diluted with 1 tablespoon milk and 1 teaspoon safflower oil
1/2 cup Citrus Glaze or Honey-Orange Glaze, page 28

Prepare the coffee-cake dough. While the dough is rising, prepare the filling.

After the dough has risen, divide it into thirds. Working with 1 portion at a time and keeping the others covered with a tea towel, roll it out on a floured surface into a 9- by 12-inch rectangle 1/4 inch thick. Spread the rectangle evenly with a third of the filling and cut into thirds lengthwise. Starting at a long edge, carefully roll up each third jelly-roll fashion and place the 3 rolls side by side. Starting in the center, braid the rolls, first to one end and then to the other. Form the braid into a circle, pinching the ends together, and transfer to a 9- or 10-inch buttered or parchment paper-lined cake pan. Repeat with remaining dough portions and filling. Let rise in a warm place until double in size.

Preheat the oven to 350°F. When the braids have risen, brush with the egg mixture and bake in the preheated oven for 30 to 35 minutes, or until nicely browned. Remove from the oven and transfer the braids to a wire rack to cool. While the braids are still warm, drizzle the glaze over.
Makes 3 braids

FRUIT OR CHEESE KUCHEN

1/3 recipe Basic Coffee-Cake Dough, page 124-125
Fresh fruit, such as halved and pitted cherries, peeled, halved and pitted apricots or plums, peeled, pitted and sliced peaches, or peeled, cored and sliced apples, or 3/4 recipe Old World Cheese Filling, page 40
1 teaspoon freshly grated lemon zest
2 tablespoons brown sugar
1/2 teaspoon ground cinnamon
1 tablespoon butter, cut in bits

Prepare the coffee-cake dough. After the dough has risen, pat it into a 9-inch parchment paper-lined or buttered and floured cake pan, building up the sides. For a fruit filling, arrange a single layer of sliced or halved fruit on top of the dough in an attractive pattern. For a cheese filling, spread the Old World Cheese Filling evenly over the dough. Sprinkle either the fruit or cheese filling with the grated zest, sugar and cinnamon and dot with the butter. Let rise in a warm place just until puffy, but not yet double in size.

While the dough is rising, preheat the oven to 350°F. Bake in the preheated oven for 45 to 50 minutes, or until golden brown. Cool slightly on a wire rack and serve warm.
Makes 8 servings

SWEDISH TEA WREATH

1/2 recipe Basic Coffee-Cake Dough, page 124-125
1 recipe Spiced Raisin Filling, page 41
1 egg, diluted with 1 tablespoon milk and 1 teaspoon safflower oil
Citrus Glaze or Honey-Orange Glaze, page 28

Prepare the coffee-cake dough. After it has risen, punch down and let rise a second time until double in bulk.

While the dough is rising, prepare the filling. Roll out the dough on a floured surface into a rectangle approximately 12 by 20 inches. Spread the filling over the rectangle and roll up from a long side jelly-roll fashion. Place on a buttered baking sheet and form the dough into a ring, pinching the ends together. With a sharp knife, cut two thirds of the way through the dough at 1-inch intervals. Turn each partially cut slice flat onto the baking sheet so that each slice slightly overlaps the one next to it. Let rise in a warm place until almost double in size, about 25 minutes.

While the dough is rising, preheat the oven to 350°F. Brush the dough with the egg mixture and bake in the preheated oven for 30 to 35 minutes, or until nicely golden. Remove from the oven and cool on a wire rack. While still warm, drizzle glaze over.
Makes 16 to 20 servings

GUALALA RIDGE COFFEE RING

Dough
1 tablespoon active dry
   yeast
2 tablespoons honey
1/4 cup lukewarm water
   (110° to 115°F)
1/2 cup plain yoghurt
1 egg, beaten
1 cup unbleached white
   flour
1 teaspoon salt
2 tablespoons butter,
   melted, or safflower oil
1-1/4 cups whole-wheat flour

Filling
1/3 cup honey
1/2 cup chopped lightly
   toasted walnuts or whole
   sunflower seeds
1/2 teaspoon ground
   cinnamon
2 tablespoons freshly grated
   orange zest
1 tablespoon fresh orange
   juice
1 banana, mashed
1/4 cup raisins

To make the dough, combine the yeast, honey and water, stir to dissolve and let stand until bubbly. Stir in the yoghurt, egg and unbleached flour, cover with a tea towel and set in a warm place until double in bulk. (This is the sponge.) When the sponge is ready, knead in the salt, butter or oil and the whole-wheat flour. Turn dough out onto a floured surface and knead until smooth and no

longer sticky, about 5 to 10 minutes. Place in an oiled bowl, turn to coat all surfaces, cover with a tea towel and let rise in a warm place until double in bulk.

Punch down and turn out onto a floured surface. Mix together all of the ingredients for the filling. Roll out the dough into a 14-inch square and spread it evenly with the filling. Starting at a long side, roll up jelly-roll fashion and cut into 1-inch slices. Arrange the slices, overlapping them, in a well-greased 8-inch ring mold. Let rise in a warm place until double in size.

Preheat the oven to 350°F. Bake in the preheated oven for about 35 minutes, or until nicely browned. Remove from the oven and invert onto a wire rack immediately. Serve warm with butter.
Makes 10 to 14 servings

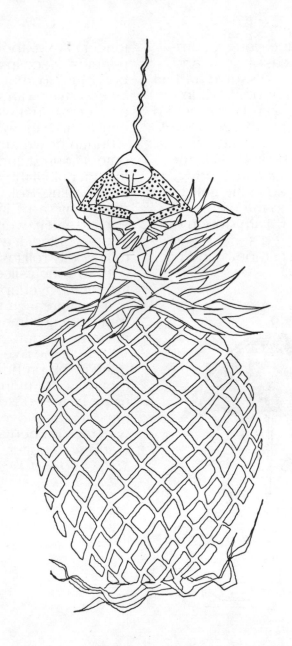

APPLE CAKE

Since this cake needs no icing because of its wonderful moistness, it travels well. In my restaurant days, I made it in large sheet pans and cut it into squares for putting in box lunches.

2 cups finely diced unpeeled
    tart green apples
1/2 cup firmly packed
    brown sugar
1/2 cup granulated white
    sugar
1 egg
1/4 cup safflower oil
2/3 teaspoon ground
    cinnamon
1/3 teaspoon ground
    nutmeg
1 teaspoon baking soda
1 cup unbleached or all-
    purpose white or whole-
    wheat flour
1/3 teaspoon vanilla
    extract
1/4 cup Apricot Glaze,
    page 27, heated, or
    confectioners' sugar
Whipped cream or plain
    yoghurt

Combine the apples with the sugars and let stand for 30 minutes or longer until the fruit juices flow freely. Preheat the oven to 350°F. Line an 8-inch cake pan or a 4- by 8-inch loaf pan with parchment paper or butter and flour it.

Whip the egg with an electric mixer until light colored. With the mixer running, slowly add the oil, then the cinnamon, nutmeg and baking soda. With a wooden spoon, stir in the flour, vanilla extract and apple mixture, blending thoroughly. Spoon the batter (it will be quite thick) into the prepared pan and bake in the preheated oven about 45 minutes, or until a wooden pick inserted in the center comes forth clean. Remove from the oven, cool in the pan on a wire rack for a few minutes, then turn out of the pan and cool completely. Top with Apricot Glaze or dust with confectioners' sugar. Serve with whipped cream or yoghurt.
Makes 8 servings

APPLE-CRANBERRY NUT CAKE

A wonderfully moist, well-textured treat for tea time, Sunday brunch or dessert.

1/2 cup safflower oil
1 cup firmly packed
  brown sugar
3/4 cup granulated white
  sugar
2 eggs
1 teaspoon vanilla extract
1 teaspoon baking soda
1 teaspoon ground
  cinnamon
1/2 teaspoon ground
  nutmeg
1 teaspoon salt
2 cups unbleached white
  flour, or
  1 cup *each* unbleached
  white and whole-wheat
  pastry flour
2 cups sliced peeled apples
1/2 cup cranberries
1/2 cup chopped lightly
  toasted walnuts

Preheat the oven to 350°F. Line a 9-inch spring-form pan with parchment paper or butter and flour it.

With an electric mixer set at medium speed, cream together the oil and sugars. Add the eggs, one at a time, beating well after each addition. Add the vanilla extract and then the baking soda, cinnamon, nutmeg, salt and flour. Lower the speed and stir in the apples, cranberries and nuts. Spoon the batter into the prepared pan and bake in the preheated oven for 45 to 50 minutes, or until a wooden pick inserted in the center comes forth clean. Remove from the oven, cool in the pan on a wire rack for a few minutes, then turn out of the pan and cool completely.
Makes 10 servings

VARIATION Substitute 1 cup honey plus 2 tablespoons frozen orange juice concentrate, thawed, for the white and brown sugars. Whip the honey and orange for 5 to 10 minutes on high speed until very light and then slowly add the oil. Proceed as directed.

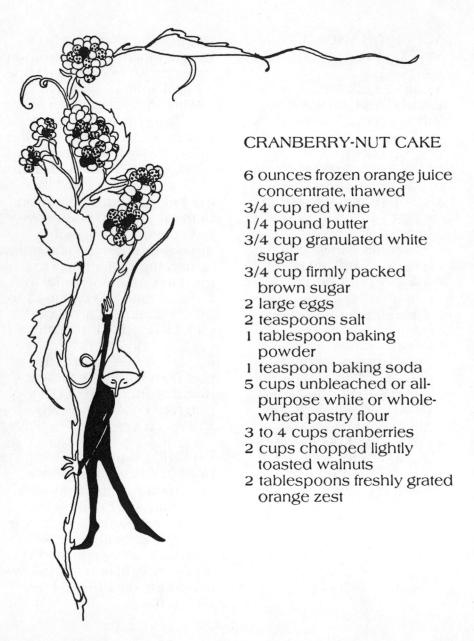

CRANBERRY-NUT CAKE

6 ounces frozen orange juice
   concentrate, thawed
3/4 cup red wine
1/4 pound butter
3/4 cup granulated white
   sugar
3/4 cup firmly packed
   brown sugar
2 large eggs
2 teaspoons salt
1 tablespoon baking
   powder
1 teaspoon baking soda
5 cups unbleached or all-
   purpose white or whole-
   wheat pastry flour
3 to 4 cups cranberries
2 cups chopped lightly
   toasted walnuts
2 tablespoons freshly grated
   orange zest

Preheat the oven to 350°F. Butter and flour two 4- by 6- by 3-inch loaf pans or two 8-inch cake pans. Combine the orange juice and wine and set aside.

With an electric mixer set at medium speed, cream together the butter and sugars until light and fluffy. Add the eggs, one at a time, beating well after each addition. Add the salt, baking powder, baking soda and flour. Then beat in the orange juice-wine mixture. Lower the speed and add the cranberries, walnuts and orange zest. Spoon the batter into the prepared pans and bake in the preheated oven for about 1 hour, or until a wooden pick inserted in the center comes forth clean. Remove from the oven, cool in the pans on a wire rack for a few minutes, then turn out of the pans and cool completely.
Makes 16 servings

CRUMB-TOPPED CAKE

2 cups whole-wheat pastry
  flour
1/2 teaspoon salt
1/4 pound butter
1/3 cup plus 2 tablespoons
  honey
2 eggs
1 teaspoon baking soda
1/2 cup buttermilk or
  plain yoghurt

Topping
1/4 cup orange marmalade
1/2 cup lightly toasted
  walnut halves
1 teapoon ground
  cinnamon
1/4 teaspoon ground
  cardamom

Preheat the oven to 350°F. Line with parchment paper or butter and flour an 8-inch square pan or a 9-inch round cake pan. In a mixing bowl, sift together the flour and salt. Add the butter, and with your fingertips, 2 knives or a pastry blender, cut it in until the mixture is the consistency of tiny peas. Mix in 2 table-spoons of the honey. Remove 1 cup of this mixture to a medium-sized bowl and add all of the topping ingredients to it, blending thoroughly. Set aside.

To the mixture remaining in the mixing bowl, add the eggs, one at a time. Then add the remaining 1/3 cup honey, the baking soda, and buttermilk or yoghurt, mixing well. Pour into the prepared pan and top with the reserved crumb mixture. Bake in the preheated oven about 30 minutes, or until a wooden pick inserted in the center comes forth clean. Cool on a wire rack.
Makes 8 to 10 servings

CRUMB-TOPPED CAKE WITH FRUIT
Before topping with the reserved crumb mixture, place a layer of sliced fruit, such as peeled apple, plum, apricot or peach slices on the batter. Use a large pan, such as a 9-inch square one. Baking time is the same.

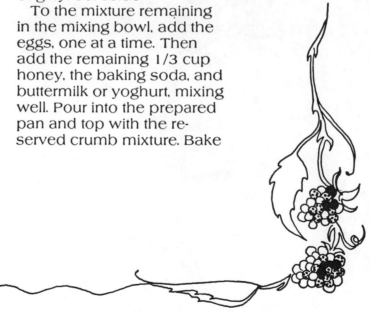

HONEY-BANANA MUFFINS

1/4 pound butter
1/2 cup honey
2 eggs
2/3 teaspoon baking soda
1/3 teaspoon salt
1/2 teaspoon vanilla extract
1/4 teaspoon almond extract
3 medium ripe bananas,
   mashed
1/4 cup plain yoghurt
2 cups sifted whole-wheat
   pastry flour
1/3 cup lightly toasted sunflower seeds or chopped
   walnuts

Preheat the oven to 350°F. Butter and flour 12 muffin-tin wells or line them with paper muffin cups.

With an electric mixer set at medium speed, cream together the butter and honey until light and fluffy. Mix in the eggs, one at a time, beating well after each addition. Add the baking soda, salt and vanilla and almond extracts. Combine the banana and yoghurt and add it alternately with the flour. Lower the speed and add the sunflower seeds or nuts. Spoon into the prepared muffin wells, filling them almost to the top. Bake in the preheated oven for 18 to 20 minutes, or until a wooden pick inserted in the center comes forth clean. They should be nicely browned when ready.
Makes 12 muffins

OL' TIME GINGERBREAD

This gingerbread is wonderful, especially on a cold winter's night in front of the fireplace. Serve it warm from the oven with lightly whipped cream (and applesauce, says Veronica). Save a taste for the dog snoozing on the hearth rug.

1/4 pound butter
1/4 cup honey, warmed
1 cup molasses
3 eggs
1/3 cup Grand Marnier
1/3 cup fresh orange juice
Grated zest of 1 orange
1/2 cup plain yoghurt
1 teaspoon baking soda
2 teaspoons ground ginger
1 teaspoon ground
  nutmeg
1 teaspoon ground
  cinnamon
1 teaspoon cream of tartar
1 cup unbleached white
  flour
1-3/4 cups whole-wheat
  plain or pastry flour
1 cup chopped lightly
  toasted walnuts

Preheat the oven to 350°F. Butter and lightly flour a 9-inch spring-form pan. With an electric mixer set at medium speed, cream the butter with the honey and molasses. Add the eggs, one at a time, beating well after each addition. Mix in the Grand Marnier, orange juice and zest and yoghurt. Add the baking soda, spices, cream of tartar and flours and mix thoroughly. Stir in the nuts and pour into the prepared pan. Bake in the preheated oven about 1 hour, or until a wooden pick inserted in the center comes forth clean. Remove from the oven and cool on a wire rack for a few minutes. Serve warm.
Makes 12 to 14 servings

PERSIMMON CAKE

My neighbor at college, Karen Hagewood, gave me this recipe in 1966. I have been looking forward to persimmon season ever since.

2 cups granulated white
  sugar
2 teaspoons safflower oil
2 cups persimmon pulp
1/4 teaspoon ground cloves
2 teaspoons ground
  cinnamon
1 teaspoon baking soda
Pinch of salt
3 cups unbleached white
  flour
1 cup milk
2 cups raisins
2 cups chopped lightly
  toasted walnuts

Preheat the oven to 325°F. Butter and flour a 10-inch tube pan or line two 8-inch cake pans with parchment paper.

Mix together the sugar and oil, then stir in the persimmon pulp. Add the cloves, cinnamon, baking soda and salt. Alternately, stir in the flour and milk until thoroughly combined. Mix in the raisins and walnuts and transfer to the prepared pan(s). Bake in the preheated oven until a wooden pick inserted in the center comes forth clean, about 1 hour if using cake pans and 1-1/2 hours if using a tube pan. Cool completely on a wire rack before removing from the pan(s).
Makes 12 to 16 servings

WHIPPED CREAM POUND CAKE

1-1/2 cups *sifted* all-purpose
   or unbleached white flour
1 cup granulated white
   sugar
2 teaspoons baking
   powder
1/2 teaspoon salt
1 cup heavy cream
2 eggs, lightly beaten
1 teaspoon vanilla extract

Preheat the oven to 350°F.
Butter and dust with sugar a
2-quart loaf pan.

   Sift the flour again with the
sugar, baking powder and
salt; set aside. Whip the cream
until stiff and stir in the eggs
and vanilla extract. Add the
sifted dry ingredients and
blend well. Pour into the
prepared pan and bake in
the preheated oven 55 minutes, or until a wooden pick
inserted in the center comes
forth clean. Transfer to a wire
rack and cool in the pan 10
minutes before turning out.
Serve warm or at room temperature.
Makes 8 to 10 servings

BANANA-NUT BREAD

The texture and flavor of this
bread improves if you can
wait at least 12 hours before
serving it.

1/2 cup safflower oil
1/2 cup granulated white
   sugar
1/2 cup firmly packed
   brown sugar
2 eggs
1 teaspoon baking soda
1/2 teaspoon baking
   powder
1/2 teaspoon salt
3 tablespoons milk
1/2 teaspoon vanilla extract
1 teaspoon ground
   cinnamon
3 medium ripe bananas,
   mashed
2 cups unbleached white
   flour, or
   1 cup *each* unbleached
   white and whole-wheat
   pastry flour
1/2 cup chopped lightly
   toasted walnuts or
   hazelnuts

Preheat the oven to 350°F.
Butter and flour a large loaf
pan.
   With an electric mixer set at
medium speed, cream together the oil and sugars. Add the
eggs, one at a time, beating
well after each addition. Add
the baking soda, baking powder, salt, milk, vanilla extract
and cinnamon. Lower the
speed and mix in the ba-
nanas, flour and nuts. Spoon
into the prepared pan and
bake in the preheated oven
approximately 1 hour, or until
a wooden pick inserted in
the center comes forth clean.
Remove from the oven, cool
in the pan on a wire rack for
a few minutes, then turn out
of the pan and cool completely.
Makes 10 to 12 servings

GINGER WHOLE-WHEAT BREAD

Although not technically a dessert, this bread is so delicious it definitely makes for a special treat with one of your homemade preserves, or with just butter anytime.

1-1/2 teaspoons granulated white sugar
1/4 teaspoon ground ginger
3 tablespoons active dry yeast
2-1/4 cups lukewarm water (110° to 115°F)
3 cups unbleached white flour
3/4 cup non-instant milk powder
1/2 cup honey
1 cup cool water
1 tablespoon salt
1/4 cup safflower oil
1 cup rye flour
1 cup yellow cornmeal
1 cup bran flakes
1/4 cup caraway seeds
1/4 cup poppy seeds
1/4 cup sesame seeds
1/2 cup sunflower seeds
3 cups whole-wheat flour
Additional unbleached white flour, as needed

Combine the sugar, ginger, yeast and 3/4 cup of the lukewarm water, stir to dissolve and let stand until bubbly. Combine the remaining lukewarm water, the unbleached white flour, milk powder and honey and stir in the yeast mixture. Cover with a tea towel and let rise in a warm place until double in bulk. (This is the sponge.) When the sponge is ready, knead in all the remaining ingredients and turn out onto a floured surface. Knead dough until smooth and elastic, about 10 to 15 minutes. Place in an oiled bowl, turn to coat all surfaces, cover with a tea towel and let rise in a warm place until double in bulk.

Punch down and divide in half. Form each half into a loaf and place in a buttered standard-sized loaf pan. Let rise in a warm place until double in size.

Preheat the oven to 350°F. Bake in the preheated oven for 35 to 40 minutes, or until nicely browned. To check for doneness, rap the bottoms of the loaves with your knuckles. If there is a hollow sound, the bread is ready. If not, return to the oven for a few minutes. Invert onto a wire rack, turn right side up and cool.
Makes 2 loaves

BROWNIES

One day I was given this recipe for fudgy, rich brownies by Jennifer Morrisey. They then became standards at the Oakland Museum Restaurant, especially among the staff. Some days I would add to their decadence with the addition of chocolate frosting.

4 ounces unsweetened
  chocolate
1/4 pound butter
4 eggs
2 cups granulated white
  sugar
1 teaspoon vanilla extract
1 cup unbleached or all-
  purpose white flour
1 cup coarsely chopped
  lightly toasted walnuts

Preheat the oven to 350°F.
Line a 9-inch square pan
with parchment paper or
butter and flour.

In the top pan of a double
boiler placed over simmering water, melt together the
chocolate and butter. Re-
move from the heat and cool
to lukewarm.

Beat together the eggs and
sugar until thickened. Mix in
the vanilla extract, flour, chocolate mixture and walnuts
until thoroughly combined.
Transfer to the prepared pan
and bake in the preheated
oven 20 to 30 minutes, or
until a wooden pick inserted
in the center comes forth
clean. Remove from the oven
and cool on a wire rack.
Makes 16 brownies

Index

Almond
  butter cookies, 116
  cake, 51
  -cheese filling, 39
  Christmas cookies, 115
  daisies, strawberry-, 49
  tart, 81
  tart, malted, 81
Amber marmalade, 48
Apple
  -blueberry conserve, 45
  cake, 130-131
  -cranberry nut cake, 131
  crisp, 108
  pie, Dutch, 88-89
  tarte des demoiselles Tatin, 87
Applesauce, 108
Apricot
  -banana filling, 38-39
  glaze, 27
  kisel, 111
  -peach preserves, 47
  preserves, 47
  sauce, 35
  tart, 84
Avocado pie, 91

Babas au rhum, 77
Bain marie, 8
Baking pans, 9-10
Baking powder, 12
Baking soda, 12
Baklava, 97
Banana(s)
  baroque, 72
  cake, 52
  cream, brandy-, 100-101
  filling, apricot-, 38-39
  muffins, honey-, 134-135
  -nut bread, 137

Baroque bananas, 72
Basic coffee-cake dough, 124-125
Basic meringue, 25
Basic pie crust, 15
Bienstitch, 125
Blueberry
  conserve, apple-, 45
  jam, 45
Bowls for mixing, 10
Brandied peach "mousse," 99
Brandy-banana cream, 100-101
Bread
  banana-nut, 137
  ginger whole-wheat, 138
Brownies, 138-139
Bûche de noël, 69
Butter
  about, 11
  cookies, 115
  cookies, almond, 116
  cookies, chocolate, 117
  strawberry-nut, 36
Butter cream
  chestnut, 31
  chocolate, 31
  custard-base chocolate, 32
  meringue-base French, 31
  mocha, 31
  praline, 31

Cake. *See also* Torte.
  almond, 51
  apple, 130-131
  apple-cranberry nut, 131
  banana, 52
  bûche de noël, 69
  carrot, 55
  cheesecake, Robert Boyle's, 94-95

cheesecake, super-rich, very
  chocolate, 96
chocolate cream roll, 66-67
chocolate decadence, 58-59
chocolate, Newport Beach, 56-57
chocolate génoise, 21
chocolate, for rolling, 22-23
cottage-cheese, 95
cranberry-nut, 132
cranberry upside-down, 53
crumb, 21
crumb-topped, 133
crumb-topped with fruit, 133
double chocolate roll, 66
gâteau au citron, 60
gâteau belle Hélène, 63
gâteau mocha, 61
gâteau montmorency, 62
gâteau Sabra, 61
génoise, 20-21
lemon génoise, 21
lemon pudding, 54
lemon-walnut roll, 64
orange-cranberry, 57
orange génoise, 21
persimmon, 136
sponge, French, 20-21
whipped cream pound, 137
Cantaloupe and peach conserve, 44
Caramel sauce, 35
Carrot cake, 55
Cheese
  filling, almond-, 39
  filling, old world, 40
  kuchen, 128

Cheesecake
    cottage cheese, 95
    Robert Boyle's, 94-95
    super-rich, very chocolate, 96
Cheesecake spread, 36
Cherry tart, fresh, 82
Chess pie, 93
Chestnut butter cream, 31
Chocolate
    about, 11
    butter cookies, 117
    butter cream, 31
    butter cream, custard-base, 32
    cake Newport Beach, 56-57
    cake for rolling, 22-23
    cheesecake, super-rich very, 96
    -cream cheese frosting, 30
    cream roll, 66-67
    decadence, 58-59
    fudge pie, 90
    génoise, 21
    glaze made with cocoa powder, 29
    glaze made with semisweet chocolate, 29
    mousse, 100
    roll, double, 66
Chou pastry, 19
Cinnamon
    buns, sticky, 126-127
    tart, 85
Citrus glaze, 28
Citrus grater, 9
Coffee cakes and rolls
    basic dough, 124-125
    bienstitch, 125
    filled braid, 127
    fruit or cheese kuchen, 128
    Gualala Ridge coffee ring, 129
    sticky cinnamon buns, 126-127
    Swedish tea wreath, 128
Coffee tortoni, 102
Cold sabayon, 102-103

Conserve
    apple-blueberry, 45
    cantaloupe and peach, 44
    cranberry, 44
    Santa Rosa plum, 44
Cookies
    almond butter, 116
    almond Christmas, 115
    butter, 115
    chocolate butter, 117
    English toffee, 118-119
    ginger, 120
    hamantashen, 120
    molasses sugar, 119
Cornucopia, from parchment paper, 10-11
Cottage-cheese cake, 95
Cranberry
    cake, orange-, 57
    conserve, 44
    -nut cake, 132
    nut cake, apple-, 131
    tart, 82
    upside-down cake, 53
Cream
    brandy-banana, 100-101
    strawberry, 105
Cream cheese frosting, chocolate, 30
Crema d'Oporto, 109
Crème caramel, 107
Crème renversée, 107
Crème pâtisserie, 38
Crumb cake, 21
Crumb-topped cake, 133
    with fruit, 133
Cumberland rum butter, Narsai David's, 32
Custard
    basic, 106
    crema d'Oporto, 109
    crème caramel, 107
    crème renversée, 107
Custard-base chocolate butter cream, 32

Double chocolate roll, 66
Double boiler, 8
Dutch pear or apple pie, 88-89

Egg-custard sauce, 33
Eggs, 11
Electric blender, 8
Electric mixer, 8
English toffee cookies, 118-119
Equipment
    basic, 9-12
    for preserving, 42-43

Figs, baked fresh, 110
Filled braid, 127
Filling
    almond-cheese, 39
    apricot-banana, 38-39
    lemon, 39
    old world cheese, 40
    pastry cream, 38
    poppy-seed, 40
    spiced raisin, 41
Flour, 11
French butter cream, meringue base, 31
French sponge cake, 20-21
Frosting. See also Butter cream.
    chocolate-cream cheese, 30
Fruit desserts
    apple crisp, 109
    applesauce, 108
    apricot kisel, 111
    baked fresh figs, 110
    fruited yoghurt, 111
    honey-baked pears, 114
    poires au vin rouge, 112-113
    spiced Italian prune plums in red wine, 113
    spiced oranges, 111
Fruit kuchen, 128
Fruit tart, 83
Fruited yoghurt, 111
Fudge pie, 90

Garnishes
    meringue mushrooms, 121
    needlethreads, 49
    praline, 49
    strawberry-almond daisies, 49
    toasted nuts, 48
Gâteau au citron, 60
Gâteau belle Hélène, 63
Gâteau mocha, 61
Gâteau montmorency, 62
Gâteau Sabra, 61
Génoise, 20-21
    chocolate, 21
    crumb, 21
    lemon, 21
    orange, 21
Ginger
    -cookie crust, 16
    cookies, 120
    whole-wheat bread, 138
Gingerbread, ol' time, 135
Glaze
    apricot, 27
    chocolate made with cocoa
        powder, 29
    chocolate made with semisweet
        chocolate, 29
    citrus, 28
    honey-orange, 28
    red currant jelly, 27
    strawberry, 27
Graham-cracker crust, 16
Gualala Ridge coffee ring, 129

Hamantashen, 120
hard sauce, 33
Honey
    about, 13
    -baked pears, 114
    -banana muffins, 134-135
    -orange glaze, 28

Jam
    blueberry, 45
    plum, 46

Kefir cheese, 13
Kirsch torte, 68
Knives, 8-9
Kuchen, fruit or cheese, 128

Lemon
    curd, 39
    filling, 39
    gâteau au citron, 60
    génoise, 21
    "mousse," 104
    -orange mousse, 105
    pudding cake, 54
    -walnut roll, 64-65
Liqueurs, 12-13

Malt syrup, 13
Marmalade, amber, 48
Measuring cups and spoons, 9
Meringue
    about, 24
    basic, 25
    japonaise, 25
    mushrooms, 121
Meringue-base French butter
    cream, 31
Mocha
    butter cream, 31
    gâteau, 61
Molasses sugar cookies, 119
Mousse
    brandied peach, 99
    chocolate, 100
    lemon, 104
    lemon-orange, 105
Muffins, honey-banana, 134-135

Narsai David's plum pudding, 79
Nectarine tart, 84
Needlethreads, 49
Nut(s). See also Walnut.
    about, 11-12
    bread, banana-, 137
    butter, strawberry-, 36
    cake, apple-cranberry, 131

cake, cranberry-, 132
    toasted, 48
    torte, German, 89

Oatmeal-honey crust, 16
Old world cheese filling, 40
Orange(s)
    -cranberry cake, 57
    génoise, 21
    glaze, honey-, 28
    preserves, quince-, 47
    spiced, 111
    syrup, spiced, 36

Parchment paper, 10-11
Pastry bag, 11
Pastry cream, 38
Pastry scraper, 9
Pâte à chou, 19
Pâte sucrée, 17
Peach
    conserve, cantaloupe and, 44
    "mousse," brandied, 99
    preserves, 47
    preserves, apricot-, 47
    sauce, 35
    tart, 84
Pear(s)
    honey-baked, 114
    pie, Dutch, 88-89
    tart, 86
    au vin rouge, 112-113
Pecan pie, 90
Persimmon
    cake, 136
    pudding, steamed, 78-79
Pie
    avocado, 91
    chess, 93
    fruit, "au naturel," 83
    fudge, 90
    pecan, 90
    sweet-potato, 92-93
    walnut, 90

Pie crust
  basic, 15
  ginger-cookie, 16
  graham-cracker, 16
  oatmeal-honey, 16
  prebaking, 18-19
  rolling out, 18-19
  sweet pastry, 17
Plum(s)
  conserve, Santa Rosa, 44
  jam, 46
  pudding, Narsai David's, 79
  in red wine, spiced Italian prune,
    113
Poires au vin rouge, 112-113
Poppy-seed filling, 40
Pound cake, whipped cream, 137
Praline, 49
Preserves. *See also* Conserve,
    Jam, Marmalade.
  apricot, 47
  peach, 47
  quince-orange, 47
Preserving, basics of, 42-43
Prebaking pie shells, 18-19
Pudding
  apricot kisel, 111
  Narsai David's plum, 79
  steamed persimmon, 78
Pudding cake, lemon, 54

Quince-orange preserves, 47

Raisin filling, spiced, 41
Raspberry purée, 34
Red currant jelly glaze, 27
Rolled cakes
  chocolate cream, 66-67
  double chocolate, 66
  lemon-walnut, 64-65
Rolling pin, 9
Rubber spatula, 9
Rum babas, 77

Sabayon, cold, 102-103
Sauce
  apricot, 35
  caramel, 35
  Cumberland rum butter, Narsai
    David's, 32
    egg-custard, 33
    hard, 33
    peach, 35
    raspberry purée, 34
    strawberry, fresh, 34
Saucepans, 10
Savarin with almonds, 76
Savarin dough, 23
Seeds, 11-12
Sinful strawberries, 70-71
Sour cream, 13
Spiced orange syrup, 36
Spiced oranges, 111
Spiced raisin filling, 41
Sponge cake, French, 20-21
  chocolate, 21
  crumb, 21
  lemon, 21
  orange, 21
Spread, cheesecake, 36
Steamed persimmon pudding,
  78-79
Stove, 10
Strawberr(ies)
  -almond daisies, 49
  cream, 105
  cream tart, 84
  glaze, 27
  -nut butter, 36
  sauce, fresh, 34
  sinful, 70-71
Streusel, 37
Sugar
  about, 13
  cookies, molasses, 119
Swedish tea wreath, 128
Sweet pastry, 17
Sweet-potato pie, 92-93
Syrup, spiced orange, 36

Tart. *See also* Tarte.
  almond, 81
  almond, malted, 81
  apricot, 84
  cherry, fresh, 82
  cinnamon, 85
  cranberry, 82
  fruit, "au naturel," 83
  nectarine, 84
  peach, 84
  pear, 86
  shell, 17
  strawberry cream, 84
Tarte
  cannelle, 85
  des demoiselles Tatin, 87
  aux poires, 86
Toffee cookies, English, 118-119
Torte
  German nut, 89
  kirsch, 68
  de Milano, 73
Tortoni, coffee, 102

Upside-down cake, cranberry, 53

Vanilla extract, 12
Vegetable peeler, 9
Virtuous vanilla, 74-75

Walnut
  pie, 90-91
  roll, lemon-, 64-65
Whipped cream pound cake, 137
Wire racks, 10
Wire sieve, 9

Yeast, 12
Yoghurt
  about, 13
  fruited, 111

Zabaglione freddo, 102-103

BIOGRAPHICAL NOTES

Veronica di Rosa, an artist and graphic designer, and Janice Feuer, a chef and cooking teacher, first combined their talents to produce a single-recipe cookbook, *Chocolate Decadence.* The spectacular success of this tiny volume prompted two other books in this dessert mini-series: *Sinful Strawberries* and *Virtuous Vanilla.* All three of these recipes are included in *Sweets for Saints and Sinners,* along with Janice's full repertoire of dessert recipes and a portfolio of Veronica's drawings.

Veronica di Rosa, a native of British Columbia, graduated in graphics and design from Vancouver School of Art and later studied at Art Center School in Los Angeles. She has worked as a copywriter and illustrator for Eaton's of Canada, was assistant editor of *About Town* magazine in Vancouver, opened Canada's first kitchen shop, and later designed four boutique shops and served as crafts buyer and manager for Woodwards department store. She presently lives among several hundred acres of grapes in California's Napa Valley with her husband, vineyardist René di Rosa.

Janice Feuer graduated from the University of California at Berkeley with a degree in communications, then received a certificate from the Cordon Bleu School of Cookery in London. Since 1971 she has taught and cooked professionally with stints at the Benson Hotel in Portland, Oregon, and Narsai's restaurant in Berkeley, where she developed many of the recipes in this book. Most recently she was pastry chef for St. Orres Inn in Gualala, a village on California's north coast. In recent years her culinary direction has changed from the rich, classic desserts of her training and early career to natural foods. The span of this interest—from sinful sweets to healthful desserts—is reflected in this book.